Developing listening skills

by Shelagh Rixon

Essential Language Teaching Series

General Editors: Roger H Flavell

Monica Vincent

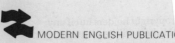

MODERN ENGLISH PUBLICATIONS

Published 1996 by
Phoenix ELT
Campus 400, Spring Way
Maylands Avenue, Hemel Hempstead
Hertfordshire, HP2 7EZ
A division of Prentice Hall International

First Published 1986 by Macmillan Publishers Ltd

Printed and bound in Hong Kong

A catalogue record for this book is available from
the British Library

ISBN 0-13-400664-X

11   10   9   8

1999   98   97   96

ACKNOWLEDGEMENTS

The author and publishers wish to thank the following who have kindly
given permission for the use of copyright material:

Cambridge University Press for an extract from *Task Listening* by
Blundell and Stokes
Pergamon Books Ltd for the extracts 'What a Business' and 'Crossed
Lines' from *ELT Documents Special—The Teaching of Listening
Comprehension Skills* by The British Council
Every effort has been made to trace all the copyright holders but if any
have been inadvertently overlooked the publishers will be pleased to
make the necessary arrangements at the first opportunity.

Contents

Introduction

This book is the product of several years spent trying to help students who were worried about learning to listen to English, and, more recently, of working with teachers who were often equally worried about *teaching* listening.

To the students my message was, 'Don't Panic! There are things you can do to improve your chances, even when you don't understand every word.' Fortunately modern published listening materials are good on the whole, and, by simply working with suitable materials, most students will develop the knowledge and strategies to make some useful progress in listening. To do this, however, they need the help of a teacher who is able to use the materials to the best advantage. This means you must have a set of effective classroom procedures and be able to use equipment (such as cassette recorders) with confidence. You should also understand the principles of why certain exercises are suggested by course books, what students' real difficulties are likely to be and how to plan listening into a year's or a term's work.

Understanding the principles also helps you to supplement published materials with your own activities, or to produce your own materials. If you have identified a need in your students which is not met by published materials, you should be able to take action that you are confident is appropriate, and that confidence comes from knowing more about the principles. What usually worries teachers is the confusing amount of jargon that has grown up around the subject of listening. Most of it concerns the material students are given for listening comprehension. Terms such as 'authentic', 'semi-authentic' and 'semi-scripted' buzz around the teaching world, often with moral overtones. 'Authentic = automatically good' is a commonly-made equation. To make matters worse, publishers and authors use these terms (and others) in conflicting and inconsistent ways. One publisher's 'authentic' means the same as another's 'simulated real speech'. I have even come across 'scripted authentic' materials! With all the confusion this creates, it is no wonder that many teachers are puzzled. I have tried to discuss these terms and others in a way that will let you look at, and listen to, teaching materials and decide for yourself what will suit your students. This may also help you if you wish to create listening materials for yourself.

I should like to acknowledge the great benefit I gained from spending three years working in the British Council's English Language Teaching Institute in London, now sadly closed-down, at a time when its staff were doing pioneering work in listening comprehension. Jim Kerr, Janet McAlpin, Marion Geddes, Gill Sturtridge, Colin Mortimer and John Hilton worked on recording techniques and types of exercise that have become widely used and have found their way into many published materials. I do not wish to underestimate the contribution of other teachers and writers during the same period, but these people provided me with my own training in approaches to listening which I believe are encouraging and useful to the majority of learners of English.

1 Real life and classroom listening

1.1 Different types of understanding

This book is about what you can do within a language course to help students understand spoken English better. The word 'understand' can have several meanings, and I shall try to cover activities and material that help the students with such aspects of understanding as:

1 Hearing all the words a speaker says
2 Understanding the plain sense of the information a speaker is giving
3 Deducing the meaning of unknown words and phrases by using the context
4 Understanding what is implied but not stated in so many words
5 Recognising a speaker's mood or attitude
6 Recognising the degree of formality with which the speaker is talking

(for the origin of this list, see Munby 1978, pp 123–131)

1.2 Different listening situations

The aim of teaching listening comprehension is (or should be) to help learners of English cope with listening in real life, but there is a large variety of different types of listening in real life. Figure 1 looks at some of the more common situations in which people living in a modern environment could need to use their listening skills.

Figure 1   Situations in which listening is important.

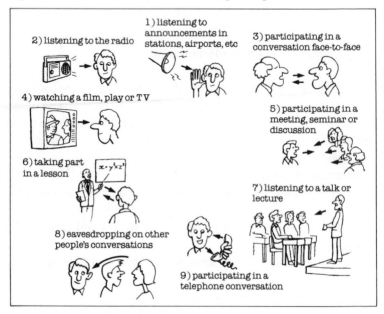

1.3 Establishing learners' priorities

If we look at Figure 1 from the point of view of the learner, it will be clear that not every situation shown will be equally relevant to every student. For example, someone who only needs to handle casual social contacts with speakers of English will be more interested in materials that involve conversational skills than in the sort of materials that could be used to develop the skills necessary for successful listening to lectures.

Not all students will have a precise set of reasons for learning English, but in many cases you will be able to draw up a rough list of the situations in which your students need, or would like, to be able to listen with success. This will be very useful as a first step to deciding what materials and exercises to choose or create.

1.4 Analysing different listening situations

Figure 2 shows some important factors affecting the difficulty of the situations illustrated in Figure 1. In real life, even though listening may be a major activity in a particular situation, the listener is usually expected to perform more than one language skill simultaneously.

Situation 3, 'taking part in a conversation', is an obvious case. Here, people need both to speak and to listen. They need to plan what to say next while they are listening, and to adjust what they say according to what other people have said. This is a very complex and demanding process. Another example is Situation 7, 'listening to a talk or lecture', which often requires the taking of notes. This requires the listener not only to understand what is being said, but to select only the important, relevant, information and reduce it to a form that can quickly be taken down in writing and remain understandable later—another complex combination of skills.

Non-native speakers of English will face additional problems when listening, due to their limited experience of the language. These difficulties affecting learners of English are summarized in Figure 3.

The fact that few situations involve 'pure' listening by itself can also be helpful. For example, the learner can often use visual clues to lend support to imperfect comprehension, as can the native speaker when, for instance, he does not hear an airport

Figure 2   Factors affecting the difficulty of listening situations.

Situation	Aids	Difficulties
1 station, airport announcements	1 visual back-up, notice boards etc 2 you can ask a member of staff for help	1 no possibility of asking speaker for clarification 2 distorted speech
2 listening to the radio	possibility of some background knowledge, eg The News	1 no possibility of asking speaker for clarification 2 no visual clues
3 participating in a conversation face-to-face	1 possibility of getting clarification from the speaker 2 visual clues – speakers' expression, gestures etc 3 the context of the situation	the need to plan your next contribution to the conversation while you are listening
4 film, play or TV	1 visual clues – speakers' expression, gestures etc 2 context of the situation	no possibility of asking speakers to clarify (and unacceptable to ask other members of audiences for too much help!)
5 meeting or seminar	1 background knowledge of subject matter 2 possibility of asking for clarification	the need to plan your contribution while listening
6 taking part in a lesson	1 the teacher <u>should</u> be trying to make himself comprehensible! 2 visual clues – black-board work etc, provided by teacher	1 the possibility of being called on to answer unexpectedly 2 understanding the contributions of other students
7 talk or lecture	1 probability of some background knowledge or expectations 2 visual clues – board work etc, provided by speaker	1 frequently the need to take notes, involving selecting important information and writing, at the same time as listening 2 interrupting for clarification not usually encouraged
8 eavesdropping	motivation (curiosity!)	you start by knowing nothing of what the conversation is about. You need to 'tune in'
9 telephone conversation	possibility of asking for clarification	1 no visual clues 2 distorted speech

Figure 3 Difficulties specific to learners of English.

Difficulties specific to language learners	Strategies learners should try
Text linguistically difficult: eg (i) words in stream of speech hard for learner to recognise (ii) certain structures unknown to learner (iii) certain words unknown to learner	Referring outside: eg using dictionary, asking for an explanation, repetition, etc Holding doubtful sections of what is heard in suspense and hoping that clarification will come later
Listener is unfamiliar with how certain types of 'spoken text' are presented and organised in the foreign culture	Mustering all pre-knowledge or expectations before listening starts Being alert to all the clues in the context or situation

announcement perfectly and looks at the departures and arrivals board to confirm what he has heard. In other cases, a speaker may use a word unknown to the listener whose meaning may be made immediately clear from the physical surroundings — if the speaker points to the thing to which he is referring, for example. Very often the listener is able to ask for a clarification or repetition if he has not understood. Often a puzzled look is enough.

In other words, real life listening not only poses problems for the learner, it also offers safety nets and extra helping factors. The exercise section (Chapters 10 to 12) offers some examples of what you can do to remind students that often they can survive very well when listening if they are prepared to make the most of all the helping factors present in the situation.

1.5 Interactional and transactional speech

The word 'conversation' can be defined as, 'any series of spoken exchanges among a small group of people in which the contributions are reasonably balanced in terms of quantity and are reasonably coherent'. However, there is clearly a difference between the main purpose of the talk that takes place between an airline clerk and a passenger wanting flight information and that between two friends exchanging greetings and enquiries about how life is treating them.

In the first case, the main concern is with obtaining or passing on concrete information. In the second, although the friends will of course also exchange some information, the main concern is with maintaining friendly social contact.

When thinking about monologue, or speech by a single person, the same distinction could be made, for example, between a boss giving his orders for the day to a group of employees, and someone recounting the events of the day to his friends, in order to amuse, or just to fill the silence.

Gillian Brown and George Yule in *Teaching the Spoken Language* (see Further Reading) distinguish these two emphases of communication. The first, the exchange of information or the use of language to 'get things done', is called *transactional*. The second, the use of language for establishing and maintaining social contact, is called *interactional*.

Many teaching materials — and not only those concerned with listening comprehension — concentrate on helping learners cope with transactional language, but it is equally important to give them the chance to recognise and use features of interactional language. In the case of listening comprehension, this means providing passages and activities which can help students with such things as recognising the speaker's emotional attitude, or the relationship between speakers (see Figure 26). Not only what is said, but the way in which it is said, is important to a correct understanding of a social situation. Students should be helped to pay attention to such things as tone of voice, volume and speed as clues to what the speaker is thinking or feeling, as well as to the actual words used. Chapter 6 looks at this aspect of listening.

The next chapter looks at the different materials that can be used for improving listening in terms of their realism or closeness to real life listening, and opens the question of how essential realism is to providing students with useful experiences.

2 Different types of listening materials

2.1 Listening for oral production or for comprehension

At this point it is important to make a distinction between the two reasons for which students may be asked to listen in their language courses:

1 To improve their understanding of the spoken word — the subject of this book.
2 To provide them with a model of the spoken language for them to imitate in oral production.

The recorded dialogue which precedes drilling of a new structure, or of examples of a language function, is the most familiar example of the second type of listening work. This is not the main consideration of this book, and it is very important to bear in mind how it differs from the passage intended for listening comprehension.

The important thing to remember is that students who are only exposed to materials intended as a basis for oral imitation will not receive adequate training in listening comprehension skills, for the following reasons:

1 The variety of language forms in teaching dialogues intended as a basis for oral practice is usually deliberately limited so that they provide several examples of the target structure or function to be taught.
2 The delivery of the speakers is usually kept fairly slow and careful — an easy and suitable model for the learner to imitate.

3 The information contained in such dialogues is usually fairly trivial and the learners are not asked to pay much attention to it. Their main concern is with the language forms.

All this is very different from what learners have to face when they start dealing with real situations and native speakers of the language. For this reason, materials that are designed to give practice in listening comprehension look (and sound) very different from most teaching dialogues.

In passages for listening comprehension work, the speakers are talking fairly quickly and naturally and the passages contain a lot of information to which the student is asked to pay attention. The main purpose of this type of listening is to help students improve their understanding of the *message* of what is said and not to introduce new language forms for their own sake.

2.2 Extensive and intensive listening

At times a person might find himself listening to something in a relaxed way, not concentrating on every word, but for the sheer pleasure of following the content of what is said. An example might be the experience of listening to an interesting or amusing radio programme, which poses no particular problems of language or difficulty of concepts. At other times the same person might find himself in a situation where he has to listen with great attention, because he is trying to pick up and remember a series of important instructions, as in the case of the employee listening to his boss's orders. Alternatively, the speaker might be using complex or unfamiliar language, as with an undergraduate listening to a lecture on a subject new to him.

The parallels between a native speaker and a learner are not exact here, but there is certainly a case for giving students the two different types of listening experience — those in which the language-level is well within their present capacity, and which therefore allow them to listen for pleasure or interest without having to make a great effort to overcome linguistic difficulties, and those in which they need to pay more attention to content and language. The first sort of experience can last quite a long time, several minutes, as in the case of easy stories read aloud by the teacher or heard on tape. They can also be quite short, when, for example, they hear a short poem or joke, just for pleasure or fun. In both cases they are not asked to do 'language work' on what they hear but have the satisfaction of an almost complete, direct, understanding of something worth hearing. This type of listening can be called *extensive* listening (by analogy with extensive reading, a term widely used in the teaching world. See Chapter 1, Williams 1984). It is an experience which it is important to give all students to keep their motivation and interest high, as well as giving them valuable extra contact with English in its spoken form. Figure 34 gives some ideas for sources of material for this purpose.

The second type of listening might be called *intensive* listening (again by analogy with reading). This is perhaps the more widely-used form of listening practice in modern classrooms. Here, the students are asked to listen to a passage with the aim of collecting and organising the information that it contains. The type of passage used is usually a little different from that used for extensive listening. It contains more concrete information, which may be quite densely packed, and often is not as easy for the students to understand on first hearing. This is because the aim is to give the students a *challenge*, to allow them to develop listening skills or knowledge of language through the efforts they make, guided by exercises or activities related to the passage. For this reason, passages for intensive listening should be short, not more than a few minutes long, because they should be played several times, straight through or in sections (usually in both ways during a lesson). This is so that students have the chance to get to grips with the contents and to have several tries at parts that at first hearing they may find difficult. Practically, the passages need to be short in order to be fit within the time-limits of a lesson, and also because of the effort that the students will be expending in their attempts to make out as much as possible. Such heavy concentration on a long passage would be extremely tiring, and would probably result in making students dislike the experience rather than finding it challenging but rewarding.

2.3 Recorded and live listening

These days, the use of recorded tapes or cassettes for listening comprehension has become standard. This has many advantages, but it is important to remember that students can also benefit from listening to the teacher or to each other in *live* listening practice. Some of the advantages and disadvantages of recorded and live listening practice are set out below:

2.3.1 *Recorded materials*

1 Recorded materials allow the non-native teacher to bring the voices of native speakers into the classroom, and allow all teachers to present a variety of voices and accents to their students.
2 When using recorded materials, the teacher or student can stop where he wishes, repeat short sections as often as he likes, and play the whole passage as often as necessary.
3 Taped materials can be used by students working on their own, either in or outside the classroom. A tape is a portable 'slice' of the English language and can be used by the student at any time.

4 Taped materials give students the chance to hear several people talking at the same time, in discussions or conversations.

5 Visual clues are not present when students listen to recorded materials on audio tape. This makes them artificial to some extent. Questions like, 'How many people are speaking?' or 'Where are they?' would not need to be considered in real life! However, this artificial removal of some of the normal information a listener would have can be used by the teacher to concentrate students' minds on the clues that they can pick up from the language itself, and can thus have positive teaching advantages. Tone of voice, the type of vocabulary used, as well as what the speakers actually say, will be thrown into more prominence, and can be made the main focus of the lesson.

6 Listening experiences based on video tape offer the advantages of audio tape, and in addition you can replay the tape to observe the use of gesture and other clues which the learner might use in real life to help with his understanding of what people are saying and of the relationships that exist between them.

7 Tapes and recorders used in the classroom are not always of a high quality. This can lead to distortion, making it difficult for students to understand the passage.

2.3.2 *Live listening*

1 Live listening experiences cannot be repeated exactly. Small sections cannot be replayed or paused in the way that recorded materials allow.

2 In compensation, they are spontaneous, and students can interact with the speaker(s) by showing their understanding (or lack of it) through expression, gesture, or simply by speaking, to ask for clarification or repetition.

3 Listeners have visual clues to help them. The speaker's gestures or use of the surrounding context can be very helpful, and many listeners find it useful to watch the speaker's mouth as he talks.

4 Some teachers who are not native speakers are worried that students may suffer from not hearing a perfect model of the language, especially in activities where the students are speaking and listening to each other. However, as mentioned above, the principal aim of listening comprehension practice is not to provide a model for oral production, but to strengthen the ability to understand spoken messages. Students can benefit from practice in reacting to what they hear, from *participating* in listening situations rather than just *overhearing* what other people are saying on tape.

Looking at the different advantages that live and recorded sources of listening experience can offer, it seems that most students will benefit from a mixed diet which will allow them to practise different strategies for coping with the spoken message.

2.4 Authentic and specially constructed materials

Most teachers want to give their students something realistic to listen to, because they want to equip them to cope with listening in real life. This has led to a great interest in so-called *authentic* materials.

Authentic listening materials consist of speech recorded in real situations, often without the speakers' knowledge at the time, so that the students are encountering a totally natural 'slice of life'.

The advantages of using materials of this type for some purposes are clear, but the teacher should also consider some possible drawbacks and limitations.

2.4.1 *Advantages of authentic materials*

1 The English heard is real, not the construction of a textbook writer or an actor's performance. This makes it both more interesting for students, and satisfying if they are able to understand what these genuine English speakers are saying.
2 Because the speech is a sample of real English, you have the scope to do work on it that a scripted, acted, listening passage might not permit. You could, for example, look at accent, tone of voice and actual expressions used, confident that you are using good linguistic data.

2.4.2 *Drawbacks of authentic materials*

1 Authentic speech is often too difficult for students at lower levels to understand except in a very superficial way. Some teachers do not object to this and favour giving students very simple tasks to do in relation to such passages. This enables them to give students at all levels experience of real English without shattering their self-confidence. However, always giving superficial or simple tasks just because the passages are beyond the students' current level of understanding, seems to be a pity. They also need the experience of being asked to get more detailed information from something they can understand more easily. This may mean using passages which are not strictly authentic, although they should not falsify the way natural English sounds.
2 Many authentic listening passages are rather too rambling and long to be used conveniently in classroom teaching (although they could have a place in self-access listening, see Chapter 14). Speakers in the real world take their time to say what they want to. They interrupt each other outrageously. They digress. They lose the thread of what they are saying. All this can provide

excellent practice for a fairly advanced learner listening in his own time, but it is rarely suitable for use with a large group of students within the time-limits of a class period. It is often more economical to use a constructed passage in which the information is more densely packed.

The controversy about authentic texts, as opposed to texts created specially for teaching purposes, seems to centre around how much reality it is possible to bring into the classroom, and which are the aspects of reality that should never be sacrificed or even compromised.

My own view is that naturalness of speech should never be sacrificed, but that it is possible to provide this in scripted or specially constructed materials as well as in authentic materials. Authentic materials can be very valuable, but authenticity is not an absolute virtue in the teaching world. The clearer focus and shorter length of many non-authentic materials can make them much more suitable for many teaching purposes. Again the compromise of giving students different types of listening seems to be the commonsense answer, with careful choice of material according to what you want the students to be able to do with it.

3 How to get the materials you need

There are three ways of obtaining suitable listening material:
1 Buying published material and using it as it stands
2 Adapting published material
3 Making your own material

The advantages and disadvantages of each possibility are considered below.

3.1 Buying published material

This is the obvious choice for most teachers and fortunately published material has improved greatly in recent years, both in terms of the naturalness of the speech heard on the tapes and of the usefulness of the exercises suggested.

Ideas tried and tested in the classroom find their way quickly into print. An example of this is jigsaw listening, which is described on page 118.

When you are selecting materials, try to obtain a sample tape from the publisher with selections of their materials. Listening to this, as well as reading what the catalogue or publicity material has to say about level, topics, type of speech and teaching approach, will give you a better feel for the material, and allow you to see how closely the material fits with the way you think your students should be working.

Because there are so many factors involved when deciding to

choose, or not to choose, particular materials, many pages could be spent on this subject. Instead of doing this I have tried to summarize the essential steps, and the factors to bear in mind, into a flow chart which appears in Figure 4. Page references are to sections of the book which take up points mentioned on the diagram and cover them in more detail.

Before you even begin to decide which material to adopt you should consider the following points:

1 Does your school have the resources to buy listening tapes and students' books. If not, do you have the time to make your own materials?

2 Is there a slot in the timetable for listening to be covered, or can you make time within your normal classes?

3 Do the materials you are considering need any special equipment or classroom arrangements? If so, can you provide this?

3.2 Adapting published material

At some points in Figure 4 the decision is not to reject imperfect teaching material but to adapt it to make it more suitable. This allows room for your own creativity without involving the enormous investment of time, skill, and effort that is required when you create your own material from scratch. When adapting, you can modify either the passage itself, or the exercises.

Some students' books still give very few exercises for each tape. Chapters 10 to 12 may give you ideas for creating extra exercises and activities that fit the potential of a particular passage.

Some units for teaching begin with exercises which may be too challenging for your students to tackle immediately. In this case, you may want to put in your own *pre-listening* exercises to provide

Figure 4 Deciding to adopt, adopt or reject material.

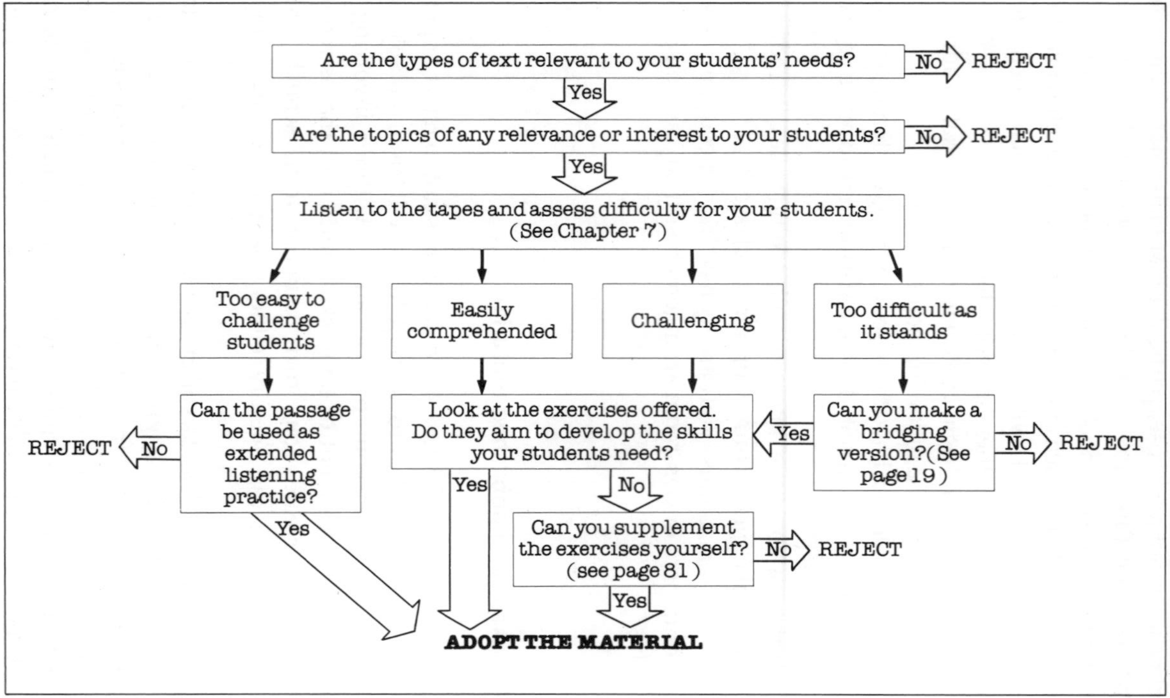

Are the types of text relevant to your students' needs? — No → REJECT
↓ Yes

Are the topics of any relevance or interest to your students? — No → REJECT
↓ Yes

Listen to the tapes and assess difficulty for your students. (See Chapter 7)

Too easy to challenge students / Easily comprehended / Challenging / Too difficult as it stands

Too easy to challenge students → Can the passage be used as extended listening practice? — No → REJECT
Yes → ADOPT THE MATERIAL

Too difficult as it stands → Can you make a bridging version? (See page 19) — No → REJECT
Yes →

Look at the exercises offered. Do they aim to develop the skills your students need?
Yes → ADOPT THE MATERIAL
No → Can you supplement the exercises yourself? (see page 81) — No → REJECT
Yes → ADOPT THE MATERIAL

a sort of bridge. In Chapter 8.2 you will find information about pre-listening work and the different purposes it can serve.

Changing the passage involves much more work than changing the exercises, and is best avoided except in cases such as that of a listening course which is very suitable on the whole, but which has one or two passages that do not succeed with your students, either because of the language used or because of the way in which the performers are speaking. In these cases there are some measures you can take:

1 If the passage is a monologue, you may be able to start the lesson with your own performance of it, using a slower, clearer delivery. This could be on tape or live. Students use this easier version to help them cope with the taped passage more confidently. The students should wait to do the exercises on the original passage.

2 If the passage involves more than one speaker you will, of course, have to record your own version if you wish to provide an easier 'bridge'. If this comes out well and sounds natural, you could decide to use your version instead of that provided by the publisher.

3.3 Making your own material

This means that you provide both listening passage and exercise material. I use the word 'provide' deliberately, because you do not always have to make your own tapes. You could also find ready-made things for students to listen to, by using radio and TV broadcasts (where copyright permits), or using commercial recordings of songs, poems, and plays — things that were not originally intended for language teaching, but whose potential you have spotted. These provide another type of authentic listening material, since they are real examples of the sort of thing that native speakers listen to.

3.3.1 *Using ready-made material*

Copyright law is strict, and schools and individuals violating it are liable to prosecution. This said, here are some points to remember when gathering materials from ready-made sources. (Technical advice about making the actual recordings appears in the Appendix.)

1 Whole radio programmes and talks are usually too long to use for listening skills training in class, although they can often be used for self-access listening (see Chapter 14). To get a suitable extract for class use, you will have to record the whole programme and then select a part of it that can stand alone. This is often less easy than it sounds, since speakers tend to make forward and backward references to other parts of the programme, making it difficult to find a section which works well independently.

2 You will need to make a transcript of your extract, for your own reference as you devise exercises to fit it, but also, in some cases, for your students to use (see the exercises on pages 109 to 111 for examples). It takes a very long time to make an absolutely accurate transcript, particularly when you are dealing with spontaneous speech. From twelve to twenty times the running length of your taped extract is the normal estimate of the time it takes a skilled transcriber. Some conventions for indicating pauses, hesitation, stammers, laughs and other features of the way the speaker is talking are given in Figure 5. They are intended to be practically useful for students rather than to represent the complete descriptive apparatus used by a linguist.

3 When you are writing exercises, it is usually much more difficult to deal with someone else's words than with a passage you have planned or created yourself. However, choosing types of listening which occur frequently and have a consistent structure will give you the chance to apply the solutions you

find more than once. An idea for exercises based on the News Bulletin, for example, can be used for all news bulletins (see Tomalin 1986).

Figure 5 Conventions used in transcribing speech for teaching purposes.

in fa-	unfinished word
and then .... he	short pause between words
(er)	any hesitation noise
(really?)	an interruption by another speaker

A <u>I don't think I</u>

B Well <u>you need to be careful</u>

underlining indicated that 2 speakers are talking at the same time

(cough)   (laugh)

the speaker laughs, coughs etc.

Example

A Yes, yes, you've pro- probably ..... probably
   eaten it many a time. You know, they (er)
   used to put it (er) in meals for schoolchildren.
   (Really?) Yes. (laugh) That's why <u>school meals</u>
   <u>were so unpopular</u> perhaps.

B <u>That's probably why I</u> <u>didn't like them</u>
   <u>much</u> <u>then</u> (laugh)

3.3.2 *Recording your own material — scripted, semi-scripted and unscripted*

In spite of the attractions of authentic materials (discussed on pages 13 to 15), texts which have been scripted or pre-planned do have a use in the classroom. You can make sure that the information you want is included, and you can plan your exercises and your listening passage together, so that they 'fit'. With authentic materials you have to accept what the **speakers** happen to say and the way they say it.

Three types of constructed listening passage will be considered: tightly-scripted, semi-scripted and unscripted.

1 *Tightly-scripted* In this format, the speakers read aloud or act out the words you have written down. Here you have absolute control over what is said, but the major pitfall is producing something that does not sound natural.

Before you record, you should have your script 'vetted' for naturalness by a native speaker, if possible. Even then, you have the problem of getting a natural *performance* from your actors. Again it is better if you can check your results with a native speaker and preferably not use the tape if it is in any way doubtful in this respect.

Some types of scripted passage present fewer problems of natural delivery than others. The mock radio talk, for example, often succeeds very well, since most real radio talks are read aloud from scripts. If you want to represent two people having a spontaneous row, however, it is probably easier to get a convincing performance not by scripting every word, but by allowing your performers the scope that semi-scripted passages provide.

2 *Semi-scripted* This is probably the ideal compromise for most teachers who want to plan some of what is to go into their tapes, but who also want spontaneity and naturalness from

their speakers. In this technique, performers are given an outline of what to say rather than a precise script.

This outline can take several forms: notes, or, with skilled performers, just a chart or a diagram containing all the information that you want them to include. Figures 6 and 7 illustrate some of the possibilities. It is best to use native speakers for this type of recording, and the same advice about having the resulting tape vetted by a native speaker applies.

Speakers working from a semi-scripted outline will produce most of the features of spontaneous speech — hesitation noises, backtracking, repetitions, false starts, etc. This will give students ample opportunity to come to grips with these aspects of spoken English, even though semi-scripted recordings are not authentic.

3 *Unscripted*   Once your actors have worked for a time from a script or semi-scripted outline, you might ask them to record the same passage once more, but this time from memory, with no script at all in front of them. **This** often produces a very good final product with added spontaneity.

Figure 6   Example of a fairly tight semi-scripted outline.

Mrs Adams saves money

Script outline for both speakers

Mrs Jones   greet Mrs Adams with surprise

Mrs Adams   return greeting and explain that you are in town just for the sales. Say you and husband needed such a lot of things that you thought you'd wait until the January sales.

Mrs Jones   ask what they wanted

Mrs Adams   a new lamp for the sitting room, the old one got broken

Mrs Jones   show interest .....

Figure 7   Very loose script outline for experienced performers.

An anthropologist looks at the High Street

Script outline for interviewer

1 Start by introducing the anthropologist to the listeners –
Dr Edward Heart of Cambridge University. Say he is the
leader of a government project to investigate behaviour of
public in crowded areas. Ask him what the purpose of the
research is (push him, surely it is going to cost a lot of
money – for what result?)

2 When he answers continue to push him – it's costing one
million pounds.

3 Let him defend himself, but try to close the interview
within 2½ minutes of the start.

Script outline for Dr Heart

1 Wait to be introduced and for the first question.

2 Facts about your project are:
>Increased violence in public places connected with
>design of buildings. It is necessary to observe people
>moving around in a scientific way, similar to observing
>monkeys.
>As a result of project, architects can design best space
>for human beings. 25 researchers on project; 50 secret
>video cameras; 5 years to complete.

If the interviewer pushes you, react indignantly.

With people with whom you work easily, you may be able to
start with no script or outline, simply discussing what is
required and then recording directly.

Another way of guiding the content of a recording without
scripting is to ask your performers a single question as a
'starter' and to record the spontaneous answers. There is often

no need to include your question on the final tape. Several different people's answers to a question such as, 'Can you describe your route to work?' or, 'Tell me about any food that you absolutely hate' can form the basis of exercises in which students compare and discuss what the speakers say.

To create materials for more advanced students, you could interview people you know have something interesting to say — visitors to the school, or friends who have interesting jobs or who have been somewhere exotic. The results can sound just as authentic as any radio interview of the same type, with the advantage that you can control the length and discuss some of the content in advance with your interviewee.

3.4 Live performances

3.4.1 *By the teacher*

This possibility is often neglected in current teaching. Apart from the possibility of reading a story in episodes for a few minutes each lesson to provide extensive listening practice, as discussed in Chapter 2.2, you can tell them a story or a joke spontaneously. You could also bring in visitors to the school and ask them to tell your class something about themselves, or about their travels or work.

You can provide intensive listening practice by speaking from notes or from a full script, or simply by giving spontaneous instructions on how to do something. A good example of this is the well-known communication exercise known as *describe and draw*. In this, one person (in this version the teacher) has a simple picture which nobody else can see. He tells the rest of the group what it looks like, giving them instructions on how to draw a picture of their own which looks as much as possible like the original. Exercises in which students follow a route on a map according to instructions are also suitable for live performances by the teacher, who gives the instructions. See Chapter 10.3 for further details on this type of exercise.

Of course, in live listening, the students will not be able to ask for an exact 'replay' of what you say, but in recompense they have the important advantage of being able to practise, in this 'face-to-face' listening, all the strategies mentioned in Chapter 1 that are useful in real-life listening. Amongst these, asking for a repetition or clarification is very important, so make sure that the students know that they are supposed to interrupt you when they are not sure of something.

3.4.2 *By the students*

The possibility of students listening to each other should not be neglected. Some teachers are worried about this, since they are afraid of students picking up each other's bad habits, but there are two arguments against this view:

1 English is now an international language, used as a lingua franca between people who do not speak it as a native language. It is thus not the *perfect* native speaker model that your students are likely to hear all the time in the real world.
2 It is not the purpose of listening comprehension practice to provide a model for students to copy in their speech. This can be done in other parts of the language course. There is more to be gained by giving learners the chance to practise interacting with another person, while trying to understand what he is saying, than there is to be lost from them not always being exposed to 'good' English speech.

Communicative activities, such as those described above, are also suitable for use by pairs or small groups of students (see Rixon 1981 for further ideas).

Jigsaw listening, described fully in Chapter 13, is another activity in which students listening to one another plays a vital part. Having listened to a tape telling part of a story, each student has the task of discussing his understanding of it with others. It is an activity which provides an excellent balance of live and recorded listening experiences for the learner.

4 Psycholinguistic theory and its implications for teaching listening

Approaches to teaching students to listen more effectively have varied over the years according to the prevalent theories on the process of listening. This chapter presents the results of some of the most recent linguistic and pedagogic research. The aim is to show the justification for particular exercise types and ways of conducting lessons, rather than to blind the reader with science. Teachers who wish to follow up any of the topics in more depth can do so by referring to the titles recommended in the Further Reading section.

4.1 The interdependence of different skills in listening

There is an everyday distinction between *hearing* something and *listening* to it. *Hearing* is simply the recognition of sounds, as when we say, 'I'm sorry, I didn't hear exactly what you said.' *Listening* implies some conscious attention to the message of what is said, as when we say, 'Are you listening to me?'

This distinction will be useful when we look at the different abilities used by a learner trying to make sense of a piece of spoken English. We shall see in Chapter 5 how many learners worry greatly about their ability to *hear* all the words, which for them is a vital part of the process of understanding the message of

Figure 8 Some components of a successful listening performance.

Global message *Level 1*	– Understanding the focus and the organisation of what the speaker is saying. – Making inferences. – Combining the sense of all the separate pieces of information in the text, so as to understand the whole message.
Grammar and vocabulary *Level 2*	– Understanding the meaning of individual pieces of information in the text. – Understanding the meaning of particular grammatical structures in the text. – Understanding the meaning of the vocabulary used in the text.
Sound system *Level 3*	– Recognising the words used by the speaker. – Distinguishing and recognising sounds correctly.

what they are *listening* to. Figure 8 looks at some of the skills necessary for successful listening, according to the traditional idea of different levels of linguistic operation. Coping with the 'building blocks' of the message — sounds and single words — is seen as a different kind of activity to understanding and combining the sense of whole pieces of information carried in the message.

In the 1950s, it was probably true to say that most teaching was based on the idea that if you taught students to cope with the separate 'building blocks' of the language — sounds, words and structures — they would put these together for themselves and become proficient in the language as a whole. In listening, effort was concentrated at the lower levels, as they appear in Figure 8. *Minimal pair* exercises, in which the student was asked to distinguish between similar-sounding words (as between 'pat' and 'pet'), were felt to be important for listening as well as for the improvement of pronunciation. Most exercises on the sense of what was said concerned the meaning of single isolated sentences. There was little attempt to help students understand the overall message of an extended piece of spoken English, or to arrive at an inference or a conclusion from what they had heard.

There are good theoretical reasons why this *parts-to-whole* approach to teaching listening is unsatisfactory if used in an extreme form (see Chapter 5, Clark & Clark 1977). It has been shown that native speakers do not rely entirely on what their ears tell them, but fill in parts of the message, usually unconsciously, according to what they *expect* to hear. This is just as well, since much of what is said in normal English speech is not said clearly in any case! Words pronounced in isolation often sound very different from the same words said in connected speech, so there is little point in concentrating too much on single words said out of context (see Chapter 5). In addition, the same sentence could have very different meanings according to what is contained in the rest of the text. It is not enough, for example, for a student to understand the superficial meaning of a sentence like, 'I didn't go home last night.' In different contexts it could mean different things. It could be an alibi, 'I wasn't there, so don't blame me!'; an excuse, 'so I couldn't phone you'; or even a confession!

Recent approaches to teaching take full account of the importance of context as shown above, and tend to adopt what might be called a more *whole-to-parts* approach. The listener is trained to try to fit everything he hears into a context, which has a number of important results in the classroom:

1 He should question anything he hears that seems to contradict or contrast with the total situation as he understands it from his listening. Jigsaw listening is one of the best techniques for bringing this about, but some ideas to use with single tapes are also given on page 95.

2 He should also try to guess the meaning of unknown words or phrases from the context before panicking or giving up in despair. Ideas for this appear on pages 102 and 103.

3 He should try to build up expectations about what he will hear, and use these to establish a framework to help him with his listening. These expectations can come either from his general knowledge or from information he has built up from what he has heard so far. Exercises on pages 98 to 101 help with this.

4 At the level of 'hearing', it has already been pointed out that much of what is said is not clearly pronounced, but that native speakers seem to experience little difficulty in disentangling the words and are not consciously aware of the 'messiness' of the signal they have to deal with. We cope so well because our strong grammatical expectations help us to fill in words or parts of words that are not clearly said. The non-native listener is obviously not so well equipped with innate grammatical knowledge, but there are exercises which both help to improve his knowledge of grammar and use the grammatical context to disentangle a 'messy' pronunciation. These appear on pages 106 to 109.

4.2 Separating or integrating listening skills in teaching

Having tried to show how listeners use skills from several levels of linguistic operation simultaneously and in an interrelated way, it may seem strange to raise the question of how they should be taught. Most realistic tasks require students to use several skills together. Getting the main information from a spoken text demands the use of the sound, the vocabulary and the sense of what is being said, as well as the ability to select and combine the relevant information from all the things that have been understood. There is, however, no harm in occasionally isolating features of language found in a listening passage to help students learn more about how the form of the language carries meaning. For example, pointing out or doing exercises on the ways speakers indicate that they wish to emphasise a point is not natural or integrated skills practice, but it is valuable if it helps students to cope better with what they listen to in future. This isolated piece of knowledge may in time become integrated into their total language competence and become something they no longer need to pay conscious attention to. Because of a wish to discourage a piecemeal approach to listening on the part of the students themselves, I tend to confine activities of this sort to the *post-listening* phase of the lesson, when the students have already achieved an understanding of the overall message of the passage and are now ready to look back and reflect on language points in it. Examples of this kind of exercise will be found on pages 103 to 105.

4.3 Narrowing the options

Experiments in which both native and non-native speakers of English have taken part show the value of exercises and activities in which the learner is given the chance to resolve any doubts he may have by using information which helps him to 'narrow the options' about what is being said.

In one experiment, a recorded phrase is said very unclearly, with a lot of background noise and other interference to make things harder. At first, the listener can make out nothing. Then he is given a small number of phrases, and is told that one of them is the phrase in the recording. He has to listen again and choose which is the correct one. Having been given this hint, he is usually able to recognise the correct phrase when he hears the recording again. On subsequent playing of the tape, he seems to 'hear' the phrase more and more easily and often ends up wondering why he found it so difficult in the first place (see Chapter 5, Clark and Clark 1977).

Experiments such as this lend support to the sort of teaching that encourages students to form their own expectations about what they will hear. This seems to help them to recognise and understand much more than if they had come to a listening passage 'cold', without any preparation. There are two main techniques, which will be illustrated in more detail in Chapter 11.1:

1 Students are told the topic of the listening passage and are asked to guess some of the words or phrases they think they might hear.

2 They are given a list of words which might possibly occur in the passage, and are asked to listen for which ones occur and which do not.

Both these techniques 'narrow the options', in that students have in mind a limited set of language items against which to match what they hear. Both techniques can notably increase the amount of language recognised at first hearing, although the first option makes more demands on the students' imagination and common sense.

4.4 Memory and listening

Steven McDonough in *Psychology and Language Learning* reports on experiments which aim to find out exactly what it is that a listener remembers of something he has heard.

It seems that, rather than remember every word, the listener summarizes the sense of what he hears as he goes along. That is, he remembers the information itself but forgets or 'purges' the exact words he hears. This lessens the overall load on the memory. Remembering six main points is much less of a strain than remembering the thousand exact words it may have taken to express these points.

Non-native speakers of a language take rather longer to go through this summarizing process than native speakers, even when their level of comprehension is good. This may account for why it is helpful to students' understanding if you pause slightly at the end of each sense-group of words. It gives a little extra time for the processing of the meaning to take place. Pausing a tape at the end of phrases and sentences often helps students a lot. They can cope with a natural speed of speech between the pauses much better than they can cope with an unnaturally slowed-down version of the same text without the pauses between the sense-groups.

When a listener has not understood the meaning of a group of words, the natural strategy is to hold the sounds or the words verbatim in his short-term memory (the type of memory you use when you need to remember something for a limited time only — a new telephone number while you are dialling it, for example). This allows the listener to return to the mysterious part and reinterpret it when, perhaps, further listening has made matters clearer. Most people will be familiar with this experience in their native language.

Learners will find themselves in this position much more often than native speakers, either because they are not quite sure of a particular section of what they have heard, or because they cannot make any sense of it at all. If there is too much to go into the short-term memory it will be put under a lot of strain and the listener will start to feel lost and may panic. Panic, of course, only makes matters worse.

Apart from the possibility of pausing, taped materials can provide a lot of support for students who are nervous about this aspect of listening. Sections which have not been understood can be repeated at will, or the whole passage played as often as the students like. This facility is, of course, artificial, since in real life such things are not possible. However, we are talking about ways of helping students *learn*, not about *testing* their current abilities. Having the chance to battle with something which at first seemed impossibly difficult and to arrive at some success in understanding it, not only gives the students the possibility of learning for themselves more about how English sounds and about the linguistic forms it contains, it also increases confidence and lessens the tendency to panic even in real-life situations. Apart from the situations in which the teacher presents the tape to the students, using a cassette or tape recorder under his or her control, it is a good idea if the students also have the chance to operate a playback machine for themselves, stopping and repeating as they wish. Mini labs, language laboratories or single recorders can be used, but it is important to train the students how to use the controls confidently and without fuss.

This section has looked at some of the justifications for the teaching approaches set out in the rest of the book. The next two chapters will look at the learners' specific difficulties with the sound of English.

5 The sound of English — the learner's fears and difficulties

5.1 Listening — the hardest skill to master?

Ask learners of English to think about the four language skills of reading, writing, speaking and listening and to put them in order of difficulty, and listening will probably come top of the list.

Many students whose general abilities in English are quite good — or so they thought — report a traumatic period after their first arrival in an English-speaking country. For quite some time — days, weeks or months, depending on the student — they can understand little or nothing of what is said to them. 'People swallow their words', 'You speak too quickly', 'How badly you pronounce your own language', are the sorts of complaint they make.

Some of the reasons for their difficulties with listening apply to all languages. Spoken words do not stay still to be scrutinised and puzzled over, as do written words. Speakers vary in the amount of consideration they show to foreigners in the clarity and care with which they express themselves. It seems, however, that there are special difficulties in coping with spoken English.

5.2 Teachers' and students' views of listening

Most teachers are concerned to help students understand the

overall meaning of what they hear, even if they do not catch every word. Many students are worried by the fact that they do not catch enough words to be confident about the overall meaning. The two different points of view are quite reasonable and need lead to no conflict, but we must all have met exaggerated forms of each attitude which are less helpful. We all know the student who panics and loses the thread of what he is listening to as soon as he misses a word, and there are many teachers who say far too casually, 'Forget about all the bits you don't understand.' What if those 'bits' add up to 75% of what is heard?

One of the main aims of this book is to find ways of giving the panic-stricken type of listener more confidence, and also some exercises and strategies to help him increase the amount of speech he can understand with ease. Teachers need to be convinced that there are exercises that can help with the 'details' of listening, and that they are worth using, and need not obscure the more communicative aim of helping the student understand the overall information or message in what he hears.

5.3 Listening difficulties stemming from pronunciation

One of the most obvious sources of difficulty for a learner of English is the way in which it is pronounced. This is an unpopular subject with many teachers and I want to get the unpleasant fundamentals over quickly! More seriously, however, it is an aspect which cannot be ignored if you want the best results from your teaching of listening.

This book cannot cover in depth all that a teacher needs to know about English pronunciation, nor can it give the practical training that is also needed. There are some excellent modern books on the subject which are readable, full of ideas relevant to developing listening skills and, in many cases, have accompanying cassettes to help the teacher sharpen his or her awareness. For some of these see Further Reading, particularly Brown, Roach, and Tench.

In this chapter, I shall briefly describe how native speakers' pronunciation of English can cause students problems in recognition, and therefore in comprehension. Intonation and expression in the voice will be covered later in Chapter 6.

There are four main sources of listening difficulty:

1 The weak relationship between English sounds and the way they are spelt in the written language.
2 Changes in sounds when they occur in rapid, connected speech.
3 The rhythm pattern of English speech.
4 Different ways of pronouncing the 'same' sound.

5.3.1 *Weak relationship between sound and spelling*

Many learners know English well in its written form, but when it comes to listening to the spoken language this experience is of little help to them. Not even a native speaker can always be sure of the correct pronunciation of a word he meets in print for the first time and, on hearing a new word, may have to look in two or three different places in the dictionary before finding it. Many learners of English fail to recognise the spoken forms of words that they 'know' very well in print or writing. The exercises on page 100 aim to help students recognise such words more easily or to note down unknown words in a way that will allow them to look for them in a dictionary or to ask someone their meaning later.

5.3.2 *Sounds in connected speech*

Many learners are accustomed to hearing a very careful, clear pronunciation of words, such as a native speaker might use when talking very emphatically or saying words in isolation. Once words are used in a connected natural utterance, some of their sounds are different to those used in very careful speech, and they may become harder for learners to recognise.

There are three main types of change in sound which cause learners listening problems:

1 *Weakening of vowels* Many words which are easy to recognise when said separately and emphatically lose this clarity when heard in connected speech. This is because, when said in isolation, their vowels receive their 'full' pronunciation, but, when they are in an unstressed position in connected speech, the vowels are weakened and are represented by the 'schwa' (or typically English 'er' sound), written as / ə / in phonetic script.

Here are some examples:

Said with stress or in isolation
you / 'juː /
to / 'tuː /
of / 'ɒv /

Said unstressed in connected speech
Will you come? / wɪl jə 'kʌm /
I've got to go / aɪv 'gɒt tə 'gəʊ /
A piece of paper / ə 'piːs əv 'peɪpə /

2 *Elision* Elision is the loss of sounds which occurs in rapid speech, as when the word 'probably' is pronounced as 'probly' / 'prɒblɪ / , or the / t / or / d / sound of the past tense marker is not pronounced as in, 'They discussed the problem.' (/ ðeɪ dɪs'kʌs ðə 'prɒbləm / instead of / dɪs'kʌs /).

A / t / might be lost at the end of other words, also, as in, 'The next day' (/ ðə 'neks 'deɪ / instead of / 'nekst /).

3 *Assimilation* This is the technical term for the way in which speakers modify their pronunciation to save effort. One example is pronouncing the phrase 'ten bikes' (/ ten baɪks / in careful speech) as / tem baɪks /

Here, the speaker, rather than making the movement from an /n/ sound, in which his tongue is touching the ridge behind his teeth, to the / b / sound, which is made with the two lips together, makes both the final sound of 'ten' and the first sound of 'bikes' using his two lips. This makes 'ten' sound like 'tem'.

These three phenomena are not variations that the native speaker introduces at random just to make things difficult for the learner. They are features which occur according to a regular pattern. One of the most fruitful and explanatory ways of looking at them is in relation to the normal rhythm of English speech.

5.3.3 *The rhythm pattern of English speech*

By 'rhythm' we mean the pattern and timing of stresses. This holds good for both music and language. In both of these one can distinguish stresses (heavy beats) from unstressed beats. In language, each beat corresponds to a syllable.

Languages are often split into two main categories — those in which the stresses tend to come at roughly equal intervals of time (to produce a regular 'tum tum' rhythm), and those in which the rhythm is less regular, with different amounts of time elapsing between the stresses.

English and other Germanic languages form part of the regular beat family of languages. Languages such as Italian and French, on the other hand, belong in the other group.

English belongs to the group of languages known technically as *stress timed*, whereas French and Italian are part of the *syllable timed* group.

These examples, taken from *Pronunciation Skills* (Tench, 1981), clearly show the nature of stress in English. Each sentence in the two groups has the same number of stresses and takes about the same amount of time to say. This is in spite of the differing number of syllables between the stresses. This is achieved by 'squashing' the intervening syllables so that they take less time to say.

| The | **man** | **smiled** | | |
| The | **man**ager | **smiled** | | |

We	**bought**	a	**book**
We have	**bought**	you another	**book**
We could have	**bought**	you another	**book**
We ought to have	**bought**	you another	**book**

This 'squashing' of unstressed syllables can cause learners a lot of trouble when they listen, for two main reasons:

1 They often find it difficult to believe that there is room for all those syllables between stresses. Even when their knowledge of grammar tells them that certain words must occur in the context, they cannot believe their ears and fail to hear them. These words get 'lost'.

2 The way in which speakers speed up on the syllables between the stresses results in their pronunciation being less clear than if they were saying the same words in isolation. Weakening of vowels, elision and assimilation all have a part to play in making this speeding up and 'squashing' possible.

5.3.4 *Different ways of pronouncing the 'same' sound*

Many teachers assume that students' listening difficulties exactly mirror their difficulties with pronunciation. Fortunately this is not entirely the case. The context usually helps learners distinguish similar-sounding words when they form part of a whole utterance. For example, even for students who could not in their own speech differentiate /iː/ from /ɪ/, 'I went to India by sheep' would be an unusual interpretation of the utterance 'I went to India by ship'!

What is more important with regard to listening to English is the student's familiarity with the range of noises which can represent the 'same' sound in English.

Take the /l/ or the /t/ sound in English. All native speakers recognise an /l/ or a /t/ when they hear one, and are often not even aware of the different pronunciations they are given in different environments. For example, in so-called Received Pronunciation, or 'BBC English', there are two ways of saying 'l'. Before a vowel at the beginning of a syllable we hear the *clear* 'l' (represented in phonetic script as /l/). At the end of a syllable, or before another consonant, we hear the *dark* 'l' (written as [ɫ] in phonetic script). Another example, which caused some of my students a problem, is the /t/ sound in English, which has several pronunciations. One of these involves a slight escape of air (aspiration) which causes a hissing noise. This is heard in Received Pronunciation at the beginning of syllables, as in 'table' ['tʰeɪbɫ] and 'till' ['tʰɪɫ] .

Some students who come from language backgrounds which have sounds similar to the English /t/, but without the aspirated variant, have found quite common words hard to recognise at first. Sometimes the slight hissing noise accompanying the aspirated /t/ has been interpreted as /st/ and I have been asked the meaning of 'steecher' when, in fact, I had said 'teacher'!

Experiences with difficulties such as these have made me take students' problems with 'hearing' just as seriously as I take their efforts to come to grips with the message of what the speaker is saying.

My main concern at this point is to consider the question of how to approach the sound-system of English with students. In this section I am including aspects relevant also to intonation, which is covered in more detail in Chapter 6. Other parts of this book will give concrete suggestions, while attempting to keep a balance between exercises concerned with helping students to 'hear' better, and those whose main focus is the message of what is said.

5.4 Implicit or explicit teaching?

Should you teach students explicitly about the sound-system of English, or should you rely on giving them more experience in listening to English, hoping that in this way they will unconsciously acquire the ability to cope for themselves with features such as elision or vowel weakening?

On the one hand, teaching the students about the subject in an abstract way will probably bore and confuse them. On the other, unless you provide them with some terms and general concepts to help them organise their experience in their own minds, they will miss many opportunities to work things out for themselves.

I have found two techniques particularly useful in helping students with 'hearing' problems:

1 Pointing out features present in the tapes they have heard.

2 Demonstrating the features that are causing difficulty.

Both are accompanied by brief comments using the terms which appear on page 44. These techniques are never used in a vacuum, that is, they are always used in response to an actual difficulty that the students have with a particular piece of spoken English, or to a specific question that someone has asked.

Pointing out is done best when using recorded materials. You can play a short section several times over, explaining what is happening, using the terms listed on page 44.

Demonstration is useful when you want to add examples of your own, after pointing something out, and also when you want to help students decipher the sounds of a particularly difficult part of a passage. Demonstration is most often done spontaneously by a teacher in class and is therefore something that native speakers may well feel more comfortable with, but it is a skill worth acquiring by all teachers, even if the non-native may prefer to demonstrate only some aspects of spoken English.

One case of demonstration serving a useful purpose from my own experience was when an entire class seemed to be having difficulty recognising the simple phrase, 'I can't come', which occurred in a taped listening passage. I demonstrated several versions of this phrase, starting with the very 'reduced' form based on the tape, and becoming progressively clearer until I arrived at a very clear emphatic pronunciation. The progression went something like this:

| / aɪ kɑ̃ː kʌm / | (the /n/ and the /t/ sounds are missing and |
| / aɪ kɑːŋ kʌm / | the vowel is nasalized) |

| / aɪ kɑːn ʔkʌm / | (all the sounds that the learner expects are |
| / aɪ kɑːnt kʌm / | present) |

I later made a quick recording of the four versions, for the students to listen to in their own time. They reported that all this had been very helpful, and one even came in a few days later, saying that he had heard and understood a slurred version of the same phrase while watching TV the previous evening.

Regular clarification and help of this kind give students both more experience and more awareness of the nature of spoken English. I use the following terms when demonstrating or pointing out pronunciation difficulties to the students:

1 *Clear/unclear*   to describe the nature of the pronunciation.
2 *Weak*   for vowels reduced to / ə /(occasionally/ ɪ / as in
  / 'mʌndɪ /·for / 'mʌndiː /).
3 *Lost sounds*, or *elision*.

4 *Stressed* and *unstressed syllables*.
5 *Change of sound* for cases of assimilation (demonstration is essential to make clear the exact change that has taken place).
6 *Going up/going down* for movement in the pitch of voice.
7 *Most prominent/important syllable* to talk about the nuclear syllable when discussing intonation (see page 48).
8 *Loud/quiet* referring to the volume of the voice.
9 *Fast/slow* referring to the speed of the speech.

Once these terms are established, stick to them and you will find that you can build up short, easily-understandable explanations.

If you use the board, your explanations will be clearer and the students will be able to take a note of them if they wish. Figure 9 shows some symbols you can use to reinforce what you say about stress, elision and pitch.

Figure 9   Some useful symbols for blackboard work on sound.

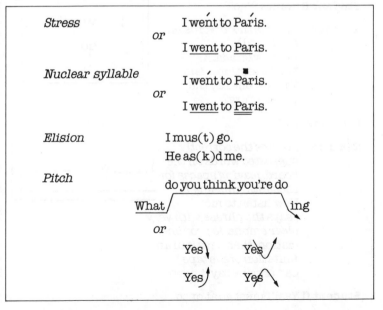

Figure 10 is an example of what might be said during the *follow-up* phase to a listening passage, when students are given the chance to ask about things that puzzled them.

Figure 10 Example of demonstration of pronunciation in a lesson.

Student	Miss, what's he saying there?
Teacher	(*replays tape until student signals that correct place is found. Replays the section causing difficulty*)
Tape	/ aɪ məs ˈgəʊ ət ˈwʌns / ('I must go at once')
Teacher	Say any words you can hear well.
Student A	'I'
Student B	'wants'? 'go'?
Teacher	(*writes these words on the board*) Now listen again. (*plays section again*) Can anyone say the phrase, now?
Students	NO!
Teacher	(*writes the correctly suggested words on the board, leaving spaces for those still missing*) Now listen to me. (*says the phrase with very clear emphatic pronunciation, then says it in an imitation of the tape*) Can anyone say it now?
Student C	Yes, 'I must go at once'

Teacher *(writes in the correctly supplied words in the spaces left on the board)*

I <u>must</u> go <u>at</u> <u>once</u>

Listen again and tell me some of the words that sound different.
(says clear version, then replays version on the tape)

Student A 'must'

Teacher Yes. On the tape the vowel is weak because the word isn't stressed, and a sound has got lost ... what sound?

must = məs(t)

Student E 't'

Teacher That's right. Now listen to the tape again. Can you hear the words more easily now?
(repeats section of tape, and continues like this)

6 More about sound — tone of voice, stress and intonation

6.1 Tone of voice

In Chapter 5, we looked at learners' difficulties in picking out sounds and identifying words within the stream of speech. Other aspects of the sound of English are also important to a correct understanding. Volume, pitch of voice, pitch range (the difference between the high notes and the low notes in a speaker's voice) and speed are amongst the important clues to a speaker's state of mind, and learners should be encouraged to take note of these things and use them to help interpret what is going on in a passage beyond the literal sense of the words themselves. An example of this type of work is given in Chapter 10, page 96, in which students are asked to interpret two different people saying the same words, 'He's a very amusing man', but meaning entirely different things. Part of the clue to this is the tone of voice. Teachers who want to follow this topic further are referred to the chapter on 'Paralinguistic Features' in *Listening to Spoken English* (Brown 1977), which is very readable and informative and, amongst other things, contains a table which helps the reader analyse for himself the different features of a pompous, a cold and a sexy way of speaking!

6.2 Stress and intonation

Some of the older-fashioned courses in listening or pronunciation try to treat the intonation of English as if it did the sort of work that I have put above under 'tone of voice', as if it provided clues to the speaker's mood or attitudes. More recent scholars such as Gillian Brown and David Brazil and his associates (see Further Reading) have questioned this, and shown convincingly that it in fact does another type of work. That is, it helps the speaker signal to the hearer how the information in his words is organised; what pieces of information are new, which are taken for granted as already known, when the speaker is changing the subject etc.

Some examples of this will be given later in the chapter, but first a brief summary of what intonation is. Again, interested readers are referred to the full treatments of the subject in books like *Listening to Spoken English* and *Discourse Intonation and Language Teaching*.

Speakers tend to talk in small 'chunks' or sense-groups. These are often separated by a slight pause. Each sense-group represents a separate piece of information. The study of intonation involves looking at what goes on inside each sense-group, in terms of stresses and the movement of the voice up or down in pitch.

Let us look at a few examples:

I love old furniture and carpets.
<u>_ _ _ _</u>   <u>_</u>

In a normal, neutral way of saying this sentence there would be four stresses, which are marked here by underlining the relevant syllables. You will remember from Chapter 5 that the stressed syllables not only sound louder, but they also are pronounced very clearly. Weakening of vowels *never* takes place on a stressed syllable.

The four stressed syllables sound more prominent than the unstressed syllables, but, of the four, one in particular stands out as most important or most prominent sounding. In the example sentence, it is the syllable 'car' of 'carpets,' so we could rewrite the sentence:

I <u>love</u> <u>old</u> <u>furniture</u> and <u>car</u>pets.

The most prominent of the stressed syllables in any sense-group is called the *tonic* or the *nuclear* syllable. In normal, neutral utterances, such as the one above, it comes in the last *information* or *content* word in the sense-group. Content words are nouns, adjectives, adverbs and full verbs. Here are some illustrations of this:

I <u>wanted</u> the <u>green</u> one.

He <u>doesn't</u> even <u>like</u> you!

Can you <u>come</u> <u>quickly</u>?

I <u>bought</u> him a <u>new</u> <u>pull</u>over.

As soon as the nuclear stress is put somewhere different in the sense-group the listener should be alert, because it means that the speaker is signalling some contrast or emphasizing a particular piece of information. Look at these two examples:

I'm <u>going</u> to <u>Pa</u>ris   (this could be a neutral answer to a question like 'What are you doing this weekend?')

<u>I</u>'m going to <u>Pa</u>ris   (this is likely to be a correction of someone's misunderstanding — perhaps the listener had thought the speaker's sister was going to Paris, and the speaker is saying, 'No, you're wrong. I am the one who's going, not my sister.')

Questions based on the understanding of this *contrastive* stress, as it is often known, used to be a favourite part of many language tests, and it is important that students should be able to cope well with it. Pointing out examples of it in your materials, and asking students to explain what the speaker means, is a practical way of incorporating this into your lesson. It could go something like this:

'Why does he say "I haven't <u>seen</u> her <u>lately</u>"?'

'Because we know he has *telephoned* her recently'

You could also occasionally demonstrate the same words said in different ways and ask students to give their interpretations, as in this example:

I <u>flew</u> to <u>Rome</u> at the <u>end</u> of <u>June</u>

I <u>flew</u> to <u>Rome</u> at the <u>end</u> of <u>June</u>

I <u>flew</u> to <u>Rome</u> at the <u>end</u> of <u>June</u>

I <u>flew</u> to <u>Rome</u> at the <u>end</u> of <u>June</u>

I <u>flew</u> to <u>Rome</u> at the <u>end</u> of <u>June</u>

So far, I have said nothing about why the nuclear syllable sounds more prominent than the others, and for the students it is not necessary to go into great detail. It is easy for most people to spot it even if they do not know how. Give them plenty of practice, little and often, in telling you which syllable they hear as the most important. You can mark it in a special way on the board, to distinguish it from other stresses. The example below shows a commonly used way of doing this.

I'm going to Paris

The reason the nuclear syllable stands out from all the others is because the speaker's voice makes a big movement in pitch on this syllable. Most descriptions of intonation pay great attention to the direction of the movement in pitch at this point, but there is no need to go into great detail here. Most students do not get on very well with detailed work on intonation patterns, and it is usually enough if they can be trained to recognise the most common pitch changes in English.

The *falling* intonation which is heard at the end of most statements, as in:

I'm going to Pa⬊ris

is one of the commonest, and students who can recognise this with ease can use it as a standard against which to compare other patterns that might be important in particular circumstances.

The *fall-rise* is also important, since it often combines with the falling intonation in a way which we shall look at in a moment. It is difficult to describe how these patterns sound, but books such as Roach, and Brazil et al (see Further Reading) have useful demonstration and exercise tapes (intended for teachers, not students), which will help resolve doubts.

Demonstration and pointing out of examples in your materials are again the best ways of getting students to recognise patterns.

6.2.1 *Recognising given and new information*

Given and *new* are technical terms used to refer to the status of any piece of information conveyed in speech or writing. *Given* information is what the speaker or writer thinks he can take for granted that his listener is already aware of. *New* information is what the speaker or writer thinks is not currently in the forefront of the minds of his audience. This could be either because they never knew about it, or because it is being presented in a new light or for the first time in this particular conversation or piece of writing.

Speakers tend to play down given information, and to highlight new information. It is important that students should be able to recognise the signals speakers provide for given and new when they are listening.

Discourse Intonation and Language Teaching is an excellent source book for teachers who wish to follow this aspect of listening in more detail. I am including a few simple examples in this book just to make the point that this aspect of intonation is very important for a full understanding of what goes on in English speech, in the hope that many teachers will want to follow it up.

Here is the same sentence said in two different ways:

I'm going to Rome after Paris

I'm going to Rome after Paris

What is the difference? There is no difference in the basic sense. In both cases we know that the speaker intends to visit two European capitals. What is different is the speaker's assumptions about what the listener already knows of his plans.

In the first, the hearer knows about the Paris plans, but not the Rome ones, so 'Rome' is highlighted as *new* information, and receives the characteristic intonation — the *high-fall*. 'Paris' is *given* information and so is played down, receiving the characteristic *fall-rise*.

In the second example, the position is reversed. The hearer knew that Rome was part of the plans, but not that Paris was. The intonation patterns are consequently reversed.

A listener eavesdropping on the conversation, coming in at this point, would be able to build up an idea of what had gone before, simply by interpreting the intonation signals correctly.

6.2.2 *Changing the subject*

Speakers also use variations in the pitch of their voices to indicate a change in subject. You can hear examples of this easily, by listening to a radio news bulletin. When the newsreader starts a new story, he raises the overall pitch of his voice (as well as speaking a little louder). This has rather the same effect as a change of key in music. The same thing happens in conversation.

When one speaker wants to introduce a new topic he changes key, although this signal is often reinforced with words like, 'By the way . . .' It is worth pointing this out to your students when it occurs in your materials, though it is not something which is likely to cause them any difficulty, since the same thing occurs in most languages (try listening to radio news bulletins in different languages and you will notice it).

6.2.3 Finished and unfinished topics

Speakers tend to keep their voices up in both volume and pitch until they have finished what they want to say. Failure to recognise this can lead to misunderstandings and unintentional rudeness, as when a non-native speaker accidentally interrupts someone because he has thought (wrongly) that the person he was talking to had finished. An example of a misunderstanding I had with a friend whose English is quite good is given below:

Friend: Well, perhaps we could meet again this evening.
Me: (*trying to be polite and say I would like to but I did not want to interfere with any other plans he had*) Fine, but I don't want to . . . (*interfere with your plans*)
Friend: (*cutting in when I had got as far as 'to'*) You don't want to? What's wrong?

It took quite some time to sort that little social disaster out!

Another important thing for students to recognise is whether or not a list is finished. Look at these two examples:

You could have tea or coffee or coke

You could have tea or coffee or coke

In the first, that is all there is on offer. In the second, the speaker has not come to the end of the things he has on offer, and the listener who does not want either tea, coffee, or coke has some reason to hope and look encouraging. In the first case, he had better make the best of things and accept one of the three alternatives quickly.

Again, you can point out examples like this in your materials or give demonstrations of the different meanings the same words can have. Understanding the words alone is a big step, but it is not the whole story.

Chapter 12.2 gives some exercises which can be used during the post-listening phase to help students reflect usefully on the characteristics of the sound of English, both in the pronunciation of individual words and the wider aspects of tone of voice, stress and intonation, as covered in this part of the book. Not all teachers may wish to use them all, but, in my experience, regular practice of this kind, providing it does not dominate over other types of listening work, can be a very useful means of helping students to interpret the message more accurately and efficiently.

7 Assessing the difficulty of listening passages

It will never be possible to find a water-tight formula for deciding how difficult a listening text is. Even reading texts are complicated to grade for difficulty, and they lack the extra dimensions present in a listening text. Quite apart from the familiarity of language structures and vocabulary, you have to consider its delivery and the speed and clarity with which it is spoken.

Moreover, it is not realistic to label any text 'easy' or 'difficulty' in a vacuum. It will always be easy for someone, more difficult for someone else, depending on the present level of language development of each person, his background knowledge of the topic and his present state of mind and body — tired, anxious people make poorer listeners, for example.

We do, however, need some rough-and-ready and commonsense guidelines to prevent us making disastrously wrong choices, and to help us to plan to give students a reasonably wide range of difficulty within a course. Challenging texts allow them to make more discoveries than easier ones, but easy texts can have a role in providing direct information to serve as input for some other task — a discussion for example — when you want the information to be quickly assimilated. Easy texts can also help to cheer up a demoralised class.

Figure 11 gives some ideas about the teaching possibilities offered by texts at different levels of difficulty (seen always in relation to students' current level).

Figure 11 Three levels of listening difficulty and their consequences for teaching.

	Immediately comprehensible	Quite easy → challenging	Too difficult
Motivation	Instant encouragement. Interesting content (hopefully).	Well-chosen exercises lead them to a sense of *success*.	Discouraging. Provokes panic.
Strategies	None needed unless distinguishing important from redundant information.	Exercises give students examples of useful strategies – guessing, writing unknown words etc.	Teacher forced to set only simple tasks. No scope for developing strategies.
Discoveries about language	Consolidation of what is already passively known.	Students will discover the meaning of previously difficult or doubtful items of language	Very few, or none if the text is impenetrable.
	SUITABLE FOR EXTENSIVE →	SUITABLE FOR INTENSIVE →	NOT RECOMMENDED

The criteria you use to decide the difficulty of a passage will, of course, overlap in real life, and you need to consider them all together. Some may even cancel each other out, as when a text which is spoken very fast and unclearly is nevertheless quite accessible to a lower intermediate student because it happens to be on a subject with which he is very familiar. However, there are certain points which should be considered when assessing a passage for listening.

7.1 Type of delivery

1 *Speed and clarity*   The features mentioned in Chapter 5 (vowel weakening, elision, assimilation) become more frequent and thickly-packed as a speaker increases his speed. This means that a listener has to cope with an acoustic signal that is actually less clear.

It is often difficult for a teacher, who is probably having no problems distinguishing the words, to develop the objectivity needed to stand back from a listening passage and judge how difficult the delivery is likely to be for his students. However, it is a skill worth paying some attention to, for their sakes!

2 *Speed and processing time*   A fast delivery also means, of course, that the information is coming to the listener at a greater speed. Chapter 4 mentioned that a learner needs more time than a native speaker to process each piece of information, even when he is having no difficulty in understanding. Any very fast delivery will therefore place an extra strain on the learner.

3 *Accent*   Everyone feels that some accents are harder than others to cope with. It is probably truer to say that some are less familiar than others, and therefore cause problems for the learner. Again, the teacher needs to listen for himself and come

to a commonsense conclusion. It is a good idea to give students experience of the range of accents that they are likely to come into contact with in real life, but extremes should be avoided, unless you know that your students are going to have to integrate into a particular community. *English Dialects and Accents* (Trudgill and Hughes, 1979), although not intended as teaching material, has some useful tapes and transcripts of speech from regions of the United Kingdom.

7.2 Density of information

1 *Differences between individual speakers* Speakers vary in how considerate they are of the people they are talking to. Some tend to say things once and once only. Others tend to rephrase, to repeat and to pause. All of this dilutes the information and gives the listener ample time to deal with it. He also has a second chance, in many cases, to pick up things he may have missed the first time they were mentioned.

2 *Differences stemming from the amount of preparation by the speaker*
Information density also varies within the speech of the same person, according to how far he has already planned in his own mind what he has to say. In a talk written to be read aloud, the information is often as densely-packed as it is in the written language. Someone speaking from notes is likely to produce something a little less dense, with re-formulations and repetitions, as he gives himself time to think.

Someone thinking as he speaks, without having been able to plan beforehand, will tend to hesitate, repeat himself and backtrack. Any dilution of information in this way will be very helpful to the learner, provided that he is alert to the opportunities it offers him.

7.3 Complexity of text

Figure 12 gives examples of the characteristics of some common types of text, and suggests how they might be put in order of complexity of organisation.

Figure 12   Some types of text organisation.

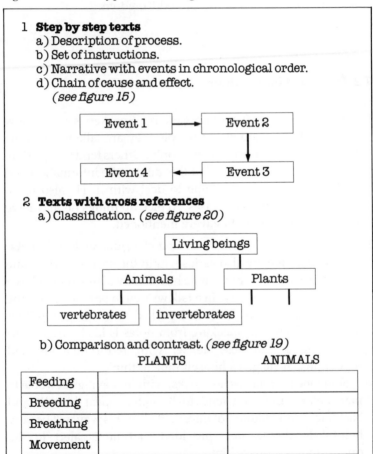

3 **Texts with cross references, back and forward references**

a) Discussion of a problem and possible solutions.
b) Detailed argument with references to points already made and yet to be made.
   (*see figure 21*)

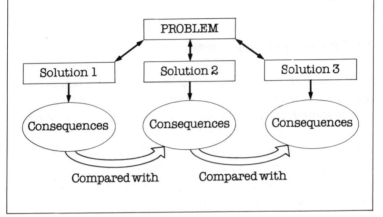

The progression is from the type of text which moves step by step, as in a narrative, a set of instructions, or a description of a process to other types of text which involve the speaker(s) making many references to different parts of the same text, both forward and backward. An example of a complexly-organised text would be one in which a problem is described, then several possible solutions are put forward and their probable consequences compared.

7.4 Number of speakers

Listening passages in which there is more than one speaker often cause more difficulty than monologues. The listeners have to relate each speaker's new contribution to what the other speakers have said, as well as to the development of the argument as a whole. At a simpler level, if a learner is listening to the radio or to audio tape, he may find it difficult to distinguish one speaker's voice from another. Conversations between different sexes are obviously easier to cope with in this respect.

7.5 Familiarity of subject matter

Even someone with a minimal grasp of a foreign language will often be able to follow a conversation or a talk on a subject that he knows something about already. He will have at the forefront of his mind a whole series of familiar concepts and ideas and will be able to use these to fill in any gaps in comprehension that might arise because of his low command of the language.

Conversely, someone with even a good command of a language may experience difficulty if he has to listen to something about a subject that is new or strange to him. This is to be expected — even native speakers suffer from this.

8 Planning a listening lesson

This chapter will cover the type of lesson whose main aim is to focus on listening skills themselves (the *intensive* listening lesson). *Extensive* listening, and lessons in which listening plays a part in a sequence of other activities, are covered in Chapters 2 and 13.

When planning a listening lesson, there are three main considerations:

1 Choosing one of the types of listening experience that you have previously identified as relevant or interesting for your students.
2 Finding exercises that both fit what the passage has to offer and practise skills connected with listening that will be useful for your students.
3 Bringing these exercises together and putting them into a sequence which forms a coherent lesson.

Chapters 10 to 12 consider types of exercise in relation to the language skills they aim to develop. This chapter looks at them in relation to the general 'shape' of a lesson, and the different stages through which it should move.

8.1 The phases of a listening lesson

A commonsense way of dividing up a listening lesson is into three phases:

1 Things to do before the students hear the passage, to help them get the most out of what they are going to hear.

2 Activities and exercises to be carried out as the students listen to the passage, to guide them as they try to grasp the main information in it.

3 Things to do once the class has come to grips with the meaning and content of the passage, and is ready to look back, to reflect on some of the language points in it, or to do some extension work based on the content of the passage.

The three phases are summarised in Figure 13, as *pre-listening*, *while-listening* and *follow-up*, and these terms will be used in the rest of the book.

Figure 13   Three phases in an intensive listening lesson.

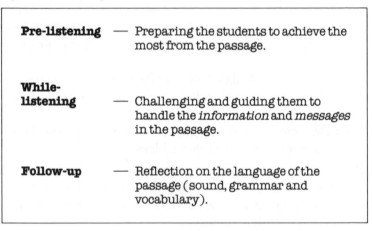

Pre-listening — Preparing the students to achieve the most from the passage.

While-listening — Challenging and guiding them to handle the *information* and *messages* in the passage.

Follow-up — Reflection on the language of the passage (sound, grammar and vocabulary).

8.2 Pre-listening

In this stage, you can set up the challenges that will give the students a reason for bothering to listen to the passage in the first place. This may involve telling them something, but not too much, about the passage and asking them to think about the sort of information they would expect to get out of a similar listening experience in real life. In the pre-listening phase, you often need to take a quick look at the exercises for the while-listening phase, to make sure that students understand the point of doing them.

Where possible, you should avoid pre-teaching the language of the listening passage, or telling students too much about the topic or the information contained in it, as this removes the challenge and interest. However, there are some cases where it pays to make sure that they are acquainted with *essential* terms or pieces of information which they would not be able to work out from the context. An example of this appears in Figure 14.

Here, the text book is wise in suggesting that the teacher should make sure that the students both know the meaning of the term 'agony column', (a regular feature in a newspaper in which readers write in with their personal problems and a sympathetic journalist tries to answer them), and have come across agony columns in their own lives. Without these two pieces of knowledge or experience, the whole point of the listening exercise will be lost, and the lesson will not proceed usefully.

In other cases, the problem may be a particular word in the passage which is used prominently or often. It may not actually be essential to following the rest of the passage, but, if from your experience with using the materials you know that it causes a 'blockage', it is better to tackle it before the passage is heard, so that students are not distracted from the rest of their listening by worrying about it.

As seen in Chapter 4, it can be very useful to get students to predict what they will hear. This helps them to recognise the actual words used in the passage. It is also useful to ask them to predict some of the content of what they will hear. This gives a wider conceptual framework against which they can match what they hear, and can lead to surprise and indignation, as when a listener expects a speaker to take a particular line of argument and he says quite the opposite. It also helps students to draw inferences from what they hear. If a piece of information which

Figure 14   Agony column.

Pre-listening	**Do you know what an *agony column* is? Who might write to one?**
Listening	**Listen to the recording twice.** **In each group of four sentences, only one is true. Put a tick (✓) in one of the boxes A, B, C or D.**

1 The radio station broadcasting the programme
   A is in Manchester. ⬚ A
   B is somewhere outside London. ⬚ B
   C is in London. ⬚ C
   D is in Berlin. ⬚ D

2 When Barry went out with his first girl friend,
   A he was under twenty. ⬚ A
   B he was over twenty. ⬚ B
   C he was no longer young. ⬚ C
   D the affair lasted a long time. ⬚ D

3 A Barry married his first girlfriend. ⬚ A
   B Barry intended to marry his girl friend, but they did not marry. ⬚ B
   C Barry never intended to marry his girl friend. ⬚ C
   D Barry and his girl friend wanted to get married but could not work out when to. ⬚ D

4 Barry had arranged with his girl friend
   A that she would return the letters and the ring. ⬚ A
   B that she would return the ring but not the letters. ⬚ B
   C that she would return the letters but not the ring. ⬚ C
   D that she would not need to return anything. ⬚ D

5 A Barry went round telling everyone about his first girl friend. ⬚ A
   B Barry started telling his wife, but stopped because she was jealous. ⬚ B
   C Barry never told his wife about the first girl friend. ⬚ C
   D Barry told his wife all about the first girl friend. ⬚ D

6 Barry's first girl friend
   A sent the letters to his wife. ⬚ A
   B was supposed to return the letters to Barry's wife, but did not. ⬚ B
   C believed that she had already sent the letters to Barry's wife ⬚ C
   D threatened to send the letters to his wife. ⬚ D

7 Barry was worried about meeting the girl
   A but he and his wife went to the pub. ☐ A
   B so he and his wife did not go to the
     pub. ☐ B
   C so he and his wife started going to the
     pub a lot. ☐ C
   D because he believed that she worked
     in the pub. ☐ D

8 Anna Tate said that Barry
   A was right in telling his wife about the
     girl. ☐ A
   B had to tell his wife about the girl. ☐ B
   C had already arranged to tell his wife. ☐ C
   D had to tell his wife that he would solve
     the problem alone. ☐ D

Follow-up

1 **Check your answers. Listen to the recording
   again. If you made mistakes, try to work out
   why.**

2 **Listen to the recording again. Every time the
   words *supposed, supposing, suppose* occur, write
   down what you hear. Can you explain the
   different meanings?**

3 **Listen to the recording again. Write down as
   many expressions as you can find which are
   colloquial and unlikely to be used in more formal
   English. Try to explain them.**

4 **Look at these sentences:**

   a) *We were to get married.*
   b) *We were to have got married.*

   **The first sentence tells us there was a plan. It
   does not tell us if the plan was carried out or not.
   The second sentence tells us there was a plan and
   the plan was not carried out.**
   **Listen to the sentences which are recorded after
   the dialogue. Put a question mark (?) if we do
   not know if the plan was carried out. Put a cross
   (X) if it was not carried out.**

   a) ☐   b) ☐   c) ☐

   d) ☐   e) ☐   f) ☐

   g) ☐   h) ☐   i) ☐

they expect to find in a passage is not there in so many words, they might start looking for ways in which the speaker might have implied it.

However, there are some passages whose whole point would be ruined if students knew too much about them before they listened. For example, if you want to give them practice in 'tuning in' — guessing what is going on by using clues in what the speakers say, as happens with eavesdropping, for example — you should start with no more introduction than something like this:

'In a moment I'm going to play you a tape. Listen and see if you can tell me where the people are and what they are arguing about. That's all you need to do the first time. Don't worry about anything else for the moment.'

8.3 While-listening

8.3.1 *Guiding students' listening*

The sort of exercise that is often used during the *while-listening* phase helps students by indicating the overall structure of the argument. A diagram, such as Figure 15, not only offers a challenge (to complete the details under each heading), but, by giving the main headings and sections of what the speaker is saying, provides a support for the learner. More advanced learners are often asked to listen for the main information without the guidance of a worksheet. It is left to them to work out the main sections of the argument and to decide which information is focal, and which is considered less important by the speaker himself.

Figure 15 Potato crisps.

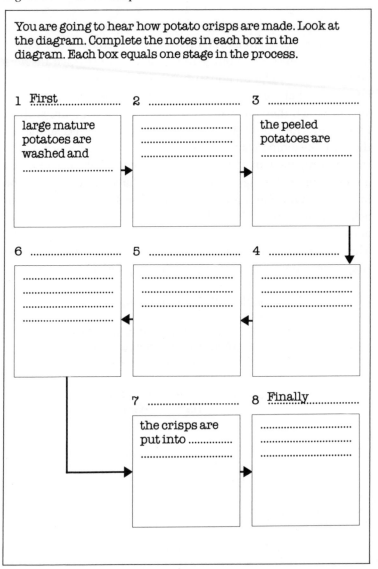

You are going to hear how potato crisps are made. Look at the diagram. Complete the notes in each box in the diagram. Each box equals one stage in the process.

1 First ....

large mature
potatoes are
washed and
....

2 ....

....
....
....

3 ....

the peeled
potatoes are

....

6 ....

....
....
....
....

5 ....

....
....
....

4 ....

....
....
....

7 ....

the crisps are
put into ....
....

8 Finally ....

....
....
....

8.3.2 *Helping students concentrate on substance*

Many students still see listening comprehension work as yet another form of grammatical or structural exercise. They expect to see questions written out as full sentences and to give answers which will be judged, not so much by the correctness of the *information* that they contain as by the correctness of the *linguistic form* in which they are expressed. However, a diagram, such as Figure 16, 'The Trouble with Harry', helps to make it clear that, at the while-listening stage, the students should not worry about interpreting long questions and producing full answers, but about demonstrating whether they have understood the important information in the passage. The simple diagram both asks the questions (Does this person like Harry or not?) and allows the student to answer them, using the minimum of words. This means that the student can concentrate on *listening*, rather than worrying about reading, writing, grammar and spelling.

Figure 16   The Trouble with Harry (version 1).

Listen to these 6 different people talking about the same person – Harry – and decide if each person likes or dislikes him. Put a tick in one of the columns to show your answer.

Speaker no.	likes Harry	dislikes Harry
1		
2		
3		
4		
5		
6		

More examples of these types of worksheets will be shown in Chapters 10 to 12.

Because the aim at this stage is for the students to understand the *message* of the text, they should not be allowed to worry too much about not catching every word. (There will be time to look at the linguistic details during the follow-up phase.) They only need to understand enough to collect the important information (as defined by the worksheets you have given them). However, this does not mean that they should content themselves with only the main gist of what is said. In many real-life situations this would be entirely inappropriate or dangerous. Imagine understanding only the gist of what a doctor told you to do with a potentially dangerous medicine, or the main drift of what your rather demanding boss had asked you to do! For this reason, I favour successive phases during the while-listening phase in which students are asked to gather more and more detailed information. A series of worksheets or a worksheet with several sections, such as that shown in Figure 26, can provide the basis for this.

8.3.3 *Types of information sought*

I have been using the word 'information' in a very broad sense, but it is important to see that it can cover a number of different things that you can ask students to find out from a passage. They could be asked to handle pure facts as in, 'fill the correct prices (dates, numbers, weights, ages, etc) on this chart.' They could also be asked to say something about the *speaker himself*, as in, 'decide if the speaker is serious or lighthearted about what he is saying', 'Does he seem to you to be confident or not about what he is telling us?' or 'Is he persuasive, or could he have been more convincing?' This kind of work relies more on the students' impression of the passage, but could lead them to a discussion in the *follow-up* of why they chose their answers, providing useful insights into the way people speak as well as into the content of what they say.

8.4 Follow-up

8.4.1 *Extension work*

In this, students take the information they have gained from the listening passage and use it for another purpose. For example, having taken notes from a passage such as 'Potato Crisps' (see Figure 15), they may want to try re-forming their notes into a written description of the process of making potato crisps. If they have been filling in a map or a chart with information during the while-listening phase, they might find it useful to try to summarize the information orally. Cases in which listening work provides an input or a stimulus to some other activity which is itself the main focus of the lesson — a simulation or a discussion, for example — will be dealt with in Chapter 13 on integrating listening.

8.4.2 *Language work based on the listening passage*

This type of work has two main focuses. Firstly, you can draw the students' attention to relevant points about the grammar and vocabulary in the listening passage. By 'relevant' I mean, 'crucial to the correct understanding or interpretation of the information', rather than features that the teacher chooses haphazardly. Some examples of exercises which pick up relevant language points are given in Chapter 11.2.

You can also make students more aware of features in the sound system of the language that are important for understanding what the speaker means. Pause, stress, use of intonation and tone of voice are all important, as are volume and speed. Students may also do work which is designed to help them recognise the words that the speaker uses more easily.

8.4.3 *Students' queries*

This type of follow-up work is based on what students themselves want to find out as a result of the lesson. If your teaching has succeeded in arousing their curiosity or making them aware of a gap in their knowledge that they want to fill, this should be counted as a success.

As students' queries are far from predictable, you have to be prepared to run the risk of not always having an answer at your fingertips. However, this does not really matter, provided your students realise that you are someone to whom they can turn without anxiety for help with their problems. If you do not have an answer immediately, you can always look it up in one of the reference sources suggested in Further Reading, and get back to your student as soon as you can, before he loses interest.

As mentioned in Chapter 5, demonstration and concrete examples are likely to be more effective than abstract explanations when you are trying to sort out a difficulty with a student.

9 Running a listening lesson

Using interesting passages and doing the right sort of exercises in a coherent sequence are essential to a successful lesson, but they are only part of the story. The overall conduct and organisation of the lesson are equally important.

You have many choices. Do you want to present a passage live or on tape? If on tape, is it best to start off by playing it all the way through, or would it be more useful to pause it? Should the presentation of the material be kept under your own control, or would it be more useful to let students listen to it by themselves in the language laboratory or in groups around separate tape recorders? Should you give them support from the written word or not? How much time should you give students to struggle with a problem by themselves before they are given a hint about the way to find the answer?

The following points are guidelines which you should follow when tackling these questions.

9.1 Variety of exercises and passages

Do not overuse any one type of exercise. If the students know, for example, that they will always start the lesson by having to listen to a tape played to them by you, answer multiple-choice questions and then move into pairs to compare their answers, this will become too much of a routine, and they will become bored and stale. Another important point is that not every listening passage is suitable for the same treatment, and you should vary your activities and exercises to suit the potential of the passage. Some will be far more suitable for students to listen to privately, in a language laboratory maybe, and others will work much better if you play small sections of them to the whole class and let the students call out their responses and reactions as you go along.

A mixture of live and recorded listening materials is preferable on most courses because of the different listening skills they can help to develop, (see Chapter 2.3). Exposure to different types of passage and to the possibilities of interaction with the speaker(s) is very important in increasing learners' experience of, and confidence in, handling the spoken word.

9.2 Helping students to see the reasons behind exercises

However scientifically you have chosen your exercises to match your students' needs, if they are allowed to do them in a blind or mechanical way they will get much less out of them than they should.

If students see the point of what they are doing, this will encourage them to use the approaches to listening that you are trying to promote, even when they find themselves in real situations. Explaining the point of exercises needs to be done with care, however. You should try to be concrete rather than technical or abstract. Which of these two explanations of the same exercise do you think would make more sense to your students?

'Exercise 9 is intended to get you used to the effect of elision of the final consonant in certain realisations of the past tenses of regular verbs'

'Exercise 9. Listen to the tape and follow the words on your tapescript. Pay attention to the past tenses of the following verbs . . . Are there any sounds missing?'

9.3 Observing students' reactions

Even if you take great care to choose your passages and activities to suit your idea of your students' needs, you cannot guarantee that all their actual difficulties and interests will be met by your lesson as planned. The most unexpected things can cause problems. On the other hand, difficulties that you anticipate can produce no trouble at all. You must be prepared to interrupt your planned sequence to cover points that are causing difficulty, or that students themselves bring up, rather than working mechanically from step one to the end of your lesson plan, with no deviations for student needs.

The possibility of covering students' queries during the follow up stage is your main safety net, but you may also have to make adjustments during the while-listening phase of your lesson. This may mean explaining a word that has not come up at the pre-listening phase, for example, but which seems to be blocking students' understanding and concentration, or pausing a tape on which the information seems to be coming too thick and fast for students to be able to process it with comfort. You may also find that you have to do much less explanation or language work during the follow-up stage than you had envisaged. In this case, reduce what you had planned to do, and do not bore students with things that do not represent any new learning or consolidation.

9.4 Allowing students time to reconsider

A lesson is not a test but a training session. It is therefore not cheating to let students hear a passage several times, in small sections, with pauses, or in any other way that is helpful to them. They should not be expected to find the answers immediately, either. Students often need time to think about their initial answers and to reconsider them. Of course, it is good occasionally to reproduce the challenges of real life inside the classroom, by letting them hear something once only, or by giving them less time to think about their answers, but the average student likes to be given the opportunity to achieve as much as he is capable of with a passage. This may take time, but it is worth it rather than to leave him with a sense of failure because he has been hurried, or has not heard the passage enough times, or in the right way for him.

It is often very useful to give the students the chance to get some of the answers, and then to listen again. The next time they listen they will already be alerted to those parts where they need to pay more attention. Perhaps they have not got some of the answers yet, or they know that other people have different answers which contradict their own. This encourages students to check their own listening, once they know that someone else has heard something different.

The best way of setting up this situation is to have a point in the lesson when students compare their answers with each other, without the teacher intervening or commenting at all on who is right or wrong. Figure 17 shows a possible sequence of steps within a lesson of this type.

Procedures like this increase the amount of communication taking place in the class. This is important, especially if doubts and comments among students are voiced in English. However, the development of oral skills is only a side benefit. The central importance of discussion in a listening lesson is that it is a means of setting up doubt and discontent among students with regard to their own answers. This motivates careful, closer, listening at the next opportunity. It may, in fact, be appropriate to allow

Figure 17 Suggested sequence of listening and discussion of answers.

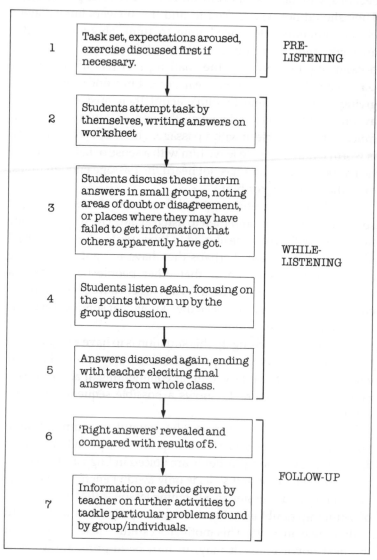

1. Task set, expectations aroused, exercise discussed first if necessary. — PRE-LISTENING

2. Students attempt task by themselves, writing answers on worksheet

3. Students discuss these interim answers in small groups, noting areas of doubt or disagreement, or places where they may have failed to get information that others apparently have got.

4. Students listen again, focusing on the points thrown up by the group discussion.

5. Answers discussed again, ending with teacher eliciting final answers from whole class. — WHILE-LISTENING

6. 'Right answers' revealed and compared with results of 5.

7. Information or advice given by teacher on further activities to tackle particular problems found by group/individuals. — FOLLOW-UP

students to discuss their answers in their native language, if this makes it easier for them to justify them or argue about the reasons for their choice.

Make sure that all the students do some listening by themselves and attempt the tasks on their own before the discussion takes place. This takes care of the worry that weaker students may rely on copying from others. The temptation to copy or to depend on other students' answers will decrease, anyway, if students realise that you do not regard the listening tasks as a form of test, and that you are far more interested in the processes that they go through to arrive at their answers than in a page full of correct but copied answers.

9.5 Preventing panic

The feeling of anxiety at impending failure often totally incapacitates a learner. This can be alleviated in several ways:

1 The idea of a lesson as a training session, not a test, should be emphasized at all costs. Students should feel that a wrong answer is not a disaster, but something whose causes can be analysed with a sympathetic teacher.

2 As mentioned in Chapter 4, recorded materials can offer their own sense of security while the student is learning to listen better, provided that he, or the teacher, is able to use the controls of the playback machine in a way that lets him hear the parts that bother or interest him as often as necessary.

3 Face-to-face listening offers the chance to interrupt and ask for clarification or repetition, and students should be trained not to be shy about this.

4 It gives the students a sense of autonomy and self reliance if you teach them ways of writing down words or phrases that they do not understand, so that they can read them back later

and ask about them or look them up in a dictionary (see page 100).

5 The teacher should always try to use listening experiences to illustrate 'reasons to be hopeful' about making sense of spoken English. This can be done by pointing out, for example, how often speakers repeat themselves, say the same thing in different ways, or explain terms they think will be unfamiliar to their audience. This will show the students how many second chances there are, if only they will calm down and make the most of the situation.

10 Listening exercises — listening for the message and information

Exercises in which students listen for information should be the focal part of any intensive listening lesson. Work on the language in the passage is also valuable, but should be kept firmly in a secondary position. Students should not be allowed to think of listening experiences merely as a means to acquiring new expressions.

Listening for information happens in the *while-listening* phase of the lesson, after the preparatory work in pre-listening, designed to help them approach the passage in the most efficient and optimistic way, and before the follow-up work, in which they reflect on the language of the passage.

Students should be encouraged to gather as much information as they can from the passage while they are listening to it, not afterwards, which would turn it into a memory test. In order to help them to do this easily, you need to provide the type of exercise mentioned on page 70, in which reading and writing is kept to a minimum, so that the students can concentrate on the task in hand — listening. Sometimes it is necessary to use written questions, as in the *true/false* exercise shown in Figure 18, but, in these cases, the questions should be read and fully understood in the pre-listening phase, before the passage is heard. Be careful not to use too many written questions at one time, or the students will not be able to remember them all as they listen. About five is the maximum for most purposes.

Figure 18   True/False questions.

The Trouble with Harry (version 2).

1. You are going to hear six different people talking about Harry. Before you listen, look at these four statements:

    a) Harry is unpopular with everyone.
    b) He is quite rich.
    c) He is generous.
    d) He is generally polite.

2. Now listen to the tape. While listening, decide if the statements above are <u>true</u> or <u>false.</u> Write <u>T</u> (true) or <u>F</u> (false) against each one.

10.1 Using charts

The two-column type of grid, shown in Figure 19, is often used as a stimulus for answers with passages in which the speaker is comparing and contrasting two things. More columns may be added if a number of things are being discussed — 4 different types of washing machine, for example. Once students become familiar with notetaking layouts like this, they may start to use them for themselves when taking unguided notes on the same types of passage.

Another type of diagram is the flow-chart illustrated in Figure 15, which is useful for guiding students' notes on stages in a story, steps in a process or sets of instructions.

Tree diagrams, such as that in Figure 20, are good for helping students to summarize passages in which different things are put into categories or classes.

Figure 21 shows a diagram in which a central problem is posed in the square box and the various solutions suggested by the speaker can be noted down in the circular boxes below.

Figure 19   Grid for comparing and contrasting two or more things.

Life in England and Italy

Look at the chart. Some of the information about England and Italy has been filled in for you.

While-listening
Listen and fill in the rest of the information.

	ITALY	ENGLAND
age at which children must start school	5	
minimum age for leaving school		16
earliest age for starting work		
earliest age for getting married		
voting age		18

10.2 Using pictures

Pictures are also a useful stimulus for students listening for information. Students can compare what they hear with the information given to them in a picture, as in Figure 22, or they can listen to a description and try to pick out the picture or pictures that the speaker is describing, as in Figure 23. They could also

Figure 20 Tree diagram for classification.

You are going to hear two people discussing different ways of losing weight. Put the key information in the correct places on the diagram. Some information has already been filled in for you.

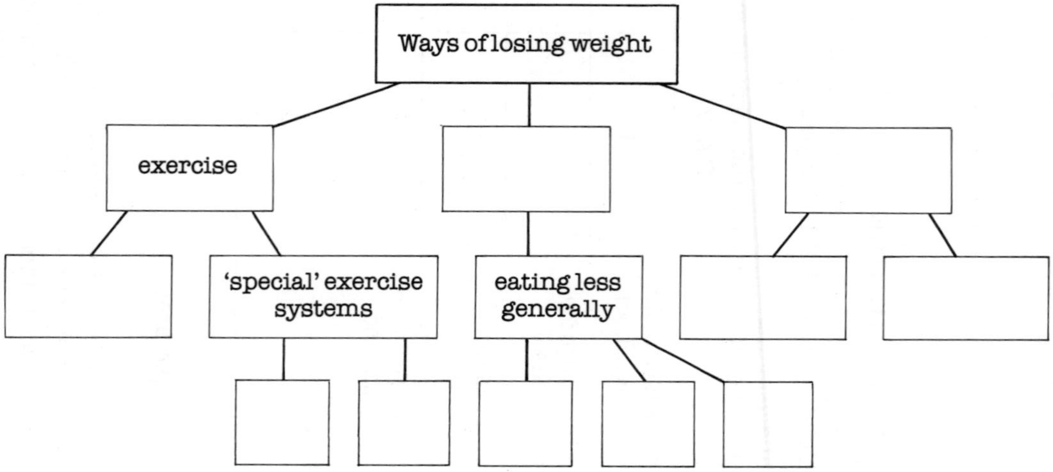

Ways of losing weight

exercise

'special' exercise systems

eating less generally

listen to a story or set of instructions which refers to a number of pictures, and be asked to recognise the pictures described and to put them into the correct order according to the passage.

Figure 21 Diagram to illustrate central problem and suggested solutions.

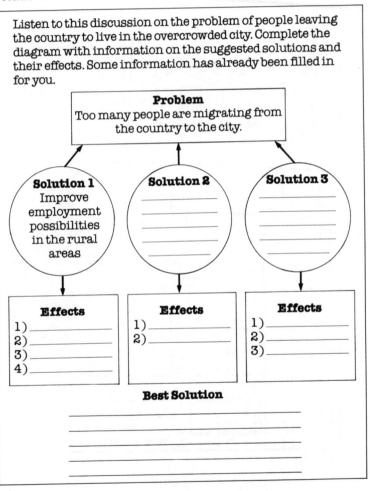

Listen to this discussion on the problem of people leaving the country to live in the overcrowded city. Complete the diagram with information on the suggested solutions and their effects. Some information has already been filled in for you.

Problem
Too many people are migrating from the country to the city.

Solution 1
Improve employment possibilities in the rural areas

Solution 2

Solution 3

Effects
1) _____
2) _____
3) _____
4) _____

Effects
1) _____
2) _____

Effects
1) _____
2) _____
3) _____

Best Solution

Figure 22 What a business.

Listen to this conversation between two businessmen whose firm sells prefabricated houses. Then study your worksheet and listen to the conversation again. This time make a note of any errors or omissions in the information given to Ted.

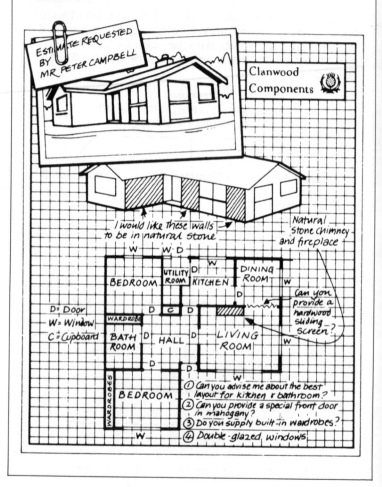

Figure 23 Culprits.

Tick the photographs of the man and woman described. Make two lists of the words that helped you make your choice, one list for the man and one for the woman.

10.3 Different types of tasks based on the message

Six types of task are summarised in Figure 24, and are described in more detail in the rest of the chapter.

Figure 24 Six types of message level tasks.

1 Following instructions correctly	
2 Matching or recognising information in a text	Concerned with the information the speakers give in so many words
3 Picking out the relevant information	
4 'Tuning in' to a passage	
5 Going beyond the literal meaning, inferences and listening ahead	Concerned with what the listener can infer, and his sensitivity to clues in accent and tone of voice
6 Recognising the speaker's mood, attitude and relationships	

10.3.1 *Following instructions correctly*

Listen and do exercises, in which students must obey instructions, can be great fun as well as providing them with immediate feedback on how good their listening has been. *O'Grady says* is a well known children's game, in which the class does what the teacher tells them: 'Put your hands on your head', 'Open your books', 'Stand up and turn round three times'. Everyone performs at once and it is easy to see who has understood well and who has not. On the other hand, since it is only a game, the tension and shame at getting something wrong are not great.

This is an example of a good type of live listening exercise for younger students.

Tracing a route on a map according to spoken instructions, or drawing a picture from a description they hear, are activities that older students, too, will enjoy.

Many communication games, designed to be played in pairs, involve the giving and understanding of instructions. This type of game also gives students practice in the interactive skills they need to be good listeners in real life. (See *How to use games in language teaching*, Rixon 1981.)

10.3.2 *Matching or recognising information in a passage*

An example of this kind of listening is shown in Figure 23, taken from *Task Listening* (Blundell & Stokes, 1981). Students have to listen and recognise the pictures described.

A more complex and demanding exercise of the same type is to give students some information before they start listening (words or pictures could be used). They then listen to see how far the information the speaker gives agrees with, or contradicts, the information they were originally given. 'What a Business!', shown in Figure 22, is an example of this.

Students can be asked during the pre-listening stage to set up their own framework of expectations, against which to match what they hear. In 'Professions', shown in Figure 25, they are asked, first of all, to name the most prestigious jobs in their own societies. They then listen to a tape which tells them about a public opinion survey on the status of different jobs in Britain. They usually get quite a few surprises at the different views various cultures have of the same job!

10.3.3 *Picking out the relevant information*

Some teachers are happy if students are able to get the gist of

Figure 25 Professions.

Pre-listening

Look at this list of different professions. Choose the two professions that have the most prestige in *your* country. Choose the one that has the least status.

architect   economist
engineer   pharmacist
doctor   lawyer
accountant   farmer
teacher

While-listening

Now listen to this passage about the results of a public opinion survey on the prestige of professions in Britain. Was your answer the same as that of the British public?

---

what is heard, and seldom go on to exercises that ask for more detailed information to be understood. I myself favour gist listening as a first stage, to give the students the framework and make sure that they are not entirely misunderstanding the situation in the passage.

I generally follow this listening, however, with exercises designed to take students down to closer detail. The sequence of exercises in 'The Trouble with Harry' (Figure 26) is an example of this. Helping students understand more than just the gist is important, not only for their motivation (they will have a greater sense of achievement), but also because it is appropriate for many listening situations. As pointed out in Chapter 2, getting the gist alone of what your boss wants is usually not enough!

Cues for collecting information can be written — direct questions or *true/false* — or can be in diagram form. At the beginning of their listening training, students may need heavy guidance as to what is the relevant information. This can be provided by the questions and charts. Later on, they should become more independent and be able to listen to a passage and decide for themselves where the important information lies. They can then make do with minimal worksheets, or no worksheets at all.

Figure 26 Information exercises at different levels.

The Trouble with Harry (version 3).

General Understanding
1. Listen to these six different people talking about the same man – Harry – and decide if each of them likes or dislikes him. Put a tick in one of the columns to show your answer. Number a) is given as an example.

Speaker no.	likes Harry	dislikes Harry
a)		✓
b)		
c)		
d)		
e)		
f)		

Understanding of More Detail
2. Now write in the reasons each speaker gives for liking or disliking Harry.

    a) irresponsible, vain, voice too loud
    b)
    c)
    d)
    e)
    f)

10.3.4 'Tuning in' to a passage

In many types of listening activity, students start off by knowing something about the passage before they hear it. This reflects many real situations. However, there are also situations in which a listener comes cold to what he hears and has gradually to 'tune in' and interpret what is going on by using clues in the text itself, rather than his outside knowledge. Eavesdropping on other people's conversations, or turning on the radio in the middle of a programme, are examples of when this happens.

Classroom activities which train students to do this include playing the first few sentences of almost any tape, without doing any pre-listening warm up. Challenge the students to work out what is going on, by using clues such as vocabulary, number of speakers and tone of voice. Students call out their ideas, which are then discussed. You can also use specially constructed materials, in which the subject matter or situation is kept deliberately mysterious until towards the end. 'Crossed Lines' (Figure 27) is an example. *Dramatic Monologues for Listening Comprehension* (Mortimer, 1980) is a brilliant collection of recordings presenting situations which are extremely puzzling at first, but which have ample clues in the speakers' words and in the way they speak, to allow the students to work out for themselves what is going on.

10.3.5 Inferences

To arrive at an inference, a listener needs to take two or more pieces of information that he has understood from the words of a text, and combine them to reach a conclusion not actually given in so many words in the passage itself. This is a much more sophisticated procedure than simply understanding single pieces of information in isolation, and it is a step that many learners

Figure 27 Crossed lines.

You are going to hear eight different people talking on the telephone but you will hear only their part of the conversation, not the part of the person they are talking to.

Listen and try to guess quickly and precisely what each conversation is about.

No 1

B

A No, I've already been.

B

A Yes, I've had it out. The appointment was at 3.15 – this afternoon, actually.

B

A No, not at all sore, just a bit numb, you know. And of course it's left the most enormous hole.

B

A Yes, I thought I'd take the afternoon off; but I should be all right by tomorrow.

B

A Yes.

B

A Oh Yes.

B

A Would I recommend him? Yes, I think I would. He's got very good hands, very skilful, and he has a nice manner. You know, gentle. And his assistant's awfully nice, especially with children. They give them each a new toothbrush when it's over.

B

A Oh. Well see you tomorrow then, Jill. 'Bye for now.

B

need to be pushed to take. Many students seem to expect much less use of implication in a foreign language than they take for granted in their own.

In order to do exercises which encourage students to draw inferences, you need passages which contain the right 'ingredients'. Take the following example:

A speaker is describing a party he hated. At one stage he says, '*I can't stand cigarette smoke*'. Later he says, '*I found it intolerable in that room*', without saying exactly why this was.

You could stop the tape at this point during the first hearing (this won't work with subsequent hearings for obvious reasons) and ask the class, '*What do you think was wrong with the room?*' Reasonable answers might be that it was crowded or noisy, but students should also remember what the speaker said about hating cigarette smoke. This should be considered as a reason. After a short general discussion, you could play the rest of the tape which reveals that the problem was indeed the smoke, as strongly suggested by the previous context.

Having a general oral discussion, sparked off by a question from the teacher, is a good way of handling the drawing of inferences. It is almost impossible to write a work sheet on inferences that does not guide the students' attention too heavily to the clues in the passage and thus give the game away at the start.

10.3.6 *Listening ahead*

A useful exercise is to ask students to predict the kind of thing they expect a particular speaker to say next, because it trains them not to passively accept everything they hear. If a speaker contradicts himself, or is inconsistent in what he says, the students should notice that something has gone wrong.

Either the listener has misunderstood part of the argument, or the speaker has gone off the rails. Students should be encouraged to ask for clarification to find out who has gone wrong.

Good passages for practice in listening ahead need to contain plenty of clues at the beginning. The speaker(s) should be expressing some strong opinion, or taking a particular line of argument. Here is an example:

The speaker is complaining about the nuisance caused by dogs on the streets. He tells of a number of unpleasant experiences.

At this point you can stop the tape and ask the students, *'What do you think he is going say next?'* One likely answer is that he will make some suggestions or recommendations about how the problem should be dealt with. (It is usual in English to follow a protest by a request or a suggestion for a remedy to the problem.) You can then ask what the students think these recommendations will be. Dogs to be banned from the streets without their owners? Leads to be worn at all times? Heavy fines for neglectful owners? Finally, you can play the rest of the tape to see how many of the predictions came true.

The important thing is not so much whether students' detailed predictions came true, but whether they were able to make the broader prediction that the indignant speaker would go on to make recommendations. If he went on to talk about the pleasures of city life, the weather or his aunt's health, the students would be right to be surprised, as would a native speaker.

A similar technique can be used with stories and jokes. Young children love joining in and trying to continue a story when the teacher pauses and says, 'and then. . . .' Adults also enjoy trying to guess the end of a story or a joke, particularly when there is some cause-and-effect sequence involved. They enjoy using their intelligence and their logical skills.

10.3.7 *Recognising the speaker's mood, attitude and relationships*

The same information can be given by different speakers or by the same speaker displaying very different moods and attitudes. For this reason, listening for these aspects of what someone says is concerned with the *message* rather than with the information in the narrow sense.

You can make your students more sensitive to tone of voice by always throwing in a few oral questions about the way speakers have delivered their information, as part of every lesson. More experience and some explanation from you should help them to make the right interpretations more often.

You could also use specially designed materials on occasions. The tape that goes with 'The Trouble with Harry' contains two people saying exactly the same words, 'He's a very amusing man'. However, one is conveying approval of Harry while the other, by putting the stress on 'amusing' and the tense voice quality, manages to convey quite the opposite, 'He's very *amusing* . . . but . . .' (More details about tone of voice have been given in Chapter 6.1.)

These six different types of tasks based on the information or message require different degrees of enterprise and independence on the part of the students, although it is not possible to impose a hard and fast grading. Obviously, it is rather less demanding to ask a student, to *recognise* information and match it with some information he is already aware of, than it is to ask him to *pick out* relevant information from a passage without preparation. Commonsense also suggests that you should not expect students to handle inference questions before they have learned to cope confidently with listening for simple points of information.

The aim of your teaching should be to bring students through the stage of competent handling of simple, obviously expressed information to a level of listening ability that allows them to interpret and evaluate what speakers say, thinking about what lies behind the words they hear, rather than about their superficial meaning.

11 Listening exercises — grammar and vocabulary in listening work

Listening comprehension work should not be done for the sake of teaching students new language, but certain types of grammar and vocabulary work can help students to be more successful with their listening. This should be kept out of the while-listening phase of the lesson, when the students' concern is with the message of the passage they are listening to, but can usefully be used during both the pre-listening and the post-listening phases.

In pre-listening, they are a way of preparing him to overcome linguistic difficulties in the passage, which might otherwise block his comprehension, or of setting up expectations about the content of the passage. When we talk of vocabulary work, it is obvious that this is very closely connected with the subject matter of the text.

In post-listening, some reflection on the language used helps to make the student more conscious of what he 'knows' (in the sense that he managed to cope with it in the comprehension tasks). It can also help him with difficulties that remain after the information and message questions have been successfully tackled. In this sense, the student may learn new language as a spin-off from his comprehension lessons.

11.1 Pre-listening work

11.1.1 *Prediction exercises — vocabulary*

Tell the students the topic of the listening passage, for example, 'You are going to hear about how potato crisps are made.' Ask them to tell you some of the vocabulary they think they might hear in a passage like this. You might get responses such as 'potato', 'cut', 'fry' and 'salt'. Perhaps some students, realising that they will be hearing about a step-by-step process, will suggest time words such as 'first', 'next' and 'then'. Accept all suggestions and write them on the board.

Students will now be able to compare this list of words with the words they actually hear in the passage — a sort of matching exercise as explained in Chapter 4. However, this is not the only benefit, since through collecting all their suggestions together, they will also have done some useful revision of vocabulary, and some students may have suggested words that were new to others. If these new words come up in the listening passage itself, it will help the students to understand and reinforce any vocabulary that might have been suggested.

11.1.2 *Prediction exercises — grammar*

If the passage is of a particular type, it may be reasonable to ask students if they can predict whether certain grammatical structures will be frequent. In the case of the 'Potato Crisps' text, it is likely that the present passive will be used a lot, since it is the description of a manufacturing process. If the students predict structures in this way, put them on the board in outline form:

THEN THE_____ $\begin{cases} \text{IS} \\ \text{ARE} \end{cases}$ _____ED

This will both remind students of important structures, and help them to recognise them if they do occur in the passage.

This type of introduction to a passage must be kept brief and light. Your aim is to encourage students to form useful expectations involving grammar and vocabulary, not to give a fully-fledged lesson on the subject.

11.1.3 *Manipulating grammar and vocabulary before listening*

This should not involve pre-teaching long lists of vocabulary or new structures. There are much more interesting, indirect approaches.

For vocabulary work, you could ask students to do a picture and word matching exercise, like that shown in Figure 28. This has two advantages. Firstly, you can bring certain words into the forefront of the students' minds (thus giving them expectations) and, secondly, you can ensure that they know of the meaning of any new words. Not all the words that appear in your picture exercise need actually appear on the tape. This will make sure that students listen more carefully to find out which of the words are included and which are not.

Figure 28   Mrs Jones' shopping list.

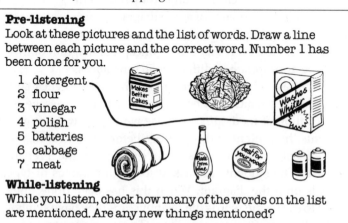

Pre-listening
Look at these pictures and the list of words. Draw a line between each picture and the correct word. Number 1 has been done for you.

1 detergent
2 flour
3 vinegar
4 polish
5 batteries
6 cabbage
7 meat

While-listening
While you listen, check how many of the words on the list are mentioned. Are any new things mentioned?

Another exercise is to give students jumbled lists of words and ask them to sort them out under different subject headings, for example, 'animals', 'furniture' and 'food'. The passage they will hear will be about only one of these topics but they will not know which it is until they hear it.

You could also give the students one-word dictations, in which they label pictures or diagrams with the words you say. This is a good way of giving them practice in writing down words that are new to them, in a way that allows them to refer back later and investigate their meaning. The spelling need not be exact as long as what they have written allows them to make reasonable reconstructions of the unknown words so that they can search for them in a dictionary or ask someone their meaning. Not every new or unusual word should be treated in this way. You should also leave some words to be guessed from the general context of the passage as the students listen.

A good way of focusing on the syntactic structures that are important to understanding a particular passage, is to give the students a diagram, such as that shown in Figure 29, and ask them to arrange a set of words on it so as to express the relationships between the things they represent.

The example shown is of a tree diagram which is often used to show how things are organised into different classes and subclasses. However, any other conceptual diagram of this sort could be appropriate to different circumstances.

In this case, the tree diagram is being used to elicit some of the structures which will be used in a listening passage on the classification of foodstuffs. Because we do not want to give the students the content of this passage before they hear it, another type of subject matter has been chosen for the preparatory exercise. The students are asked to put the names of types of animals onto the diagram. When this has been done, they are asked to express in words the relationships they have symbolised on the diagram. Structures such as, 'There are two types of ——'

Figure 29 Classification.

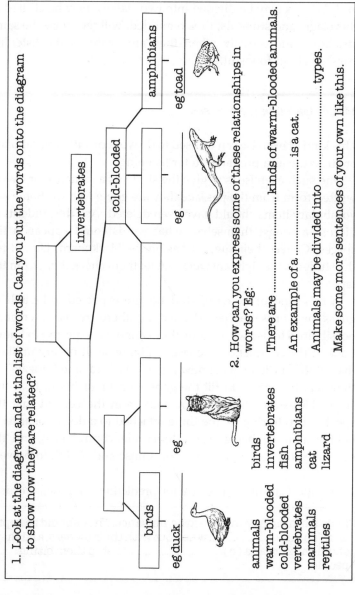

1. Look at the diagram and at the list of words. Can you put the words onto the diagram to show how they are related?

birds
invertebrates
fish
amphibians
cat
lizard

animals
warm-blooded
cold-blooded
vertebrates
mammals
reptiles

2. How can you express some of these relationships in words? Eg:

There are .... kinds of warm-blooded animals.

An example of a .... is a cat.

Animals may be divided into .... types.

Make some more sentences of your own like this.

and, '————s may be divided into two classes' may be elicited at this stage, and students, thus reminded, will recognise the same structures more easily when they are heard in the listening passage about foodstuffs.

11.1.4 *Gap-filling exercises*

This kind of exercise can be used to do work on either vocabulary or structure as a preparation for listening.

One such exercise is to give the students a sentence or two in written form from the passage they are going to hear. Some key vocabulary items should have been deleted. Ask the students to discuss amongst themselves what words could appear in the spaces. Collect their suggestions on the blackboard. Do not tell the students the right answers, but let them check them from the tape.

In this kind of exercise, students are expected to be able to guess the words you have deleted, but there are also interesting possibilities to use with words they cannot be expected to know. Look at the completion exercise in Figure 30. It is very unlikely that all the students will know the words 'lead' and 'muzzle', so they will be unable to fill the gaps with English words at this stage. However, it is fairly obvious from the context that the speaker is referring to 'the thing attached to a dog's collar to be held by a human being to keep him under control' in a), and 'the cage-like structure put over a dog's nose and mouth to prevent

Figure 30 Gap-filling exercise for predicting unknown words.

Dogs running free in town are a nuisance. They should be kept on a (a) .... when out with their owners, and they should also wear a (b) .... to stop them biting people.

him biting' in b). The learner will know what is meant although he cannot supply the English words. Play the passage and let the students listen for themselves to find out what the words are in English.

Work like this is valuable in preparing students to guess meaning from context when they hear a new word. Giving them time to think, which is provided in these exercises by letting them *read* the extract before *hearing* it, is an intermediate step towards asking them to guess directly from something they hear. Intermediate steps like this are helpful in boosting the confidence of students who are inclined to panic if they are thrown straight into a listening passage containing unknown words.

Completion exercises involving grammatical structures (pronouns, articles, prepositions etc) have been included in the section on pronunciation in Chapter 12, because they are more relevant to helping students cope with unstressed syllables.

11.2 Follow-up work

Students who have successfully coped with the comprehension tasks on a passage during the while-listening phase, are in a good position to look at the form in which the messages in the passage are expressed.

It is very useful if you bring together for the students sets of vocabulary items or phrases that are used in a particular area of meaning, for example:

all the expressions connected with cause that are used in a particular passage.

all the words and phrases to do with sequence in time.

all the favourable and all the unfavourable adjectives used about Harry in 'The Trouble with Harry' (see Figure 26).

all the expressions used to show speaker's certainty or doubt (see Figure 31).

Figure 31   Follow-up work.

How long can human beings live?

Listen to this conversation about some of the oldest people in the world. Complete the chart while you listen. Leave column 4 until you have completed the rest of the chart.

| | While-listening | | | Follow-up |
	Place	Name of old person (if given)	Age	How sure is the speaker that the age given is correct? Write down his words.
1.	Japan			
2.				
3.			127	
4.				
5.	Georgia			
6.				

When you are collecting expressions like these, it is a good idea to work orally, with all the students contributing their suggestions. Put headings like 'Time words' on the board and write up all the contributions under the appropriate headings.

You can collect ideas at a number of stages. First, put up the heading(s) you need. Then ask students if they can remember anything to contribute without hearing the tape again. Collect their offerings on the board. Then play the tape right through, asking students to put up their hands and stop you when they hear something to add to the list. Pause the tape and replay as necessary. Go back through the tape, picking up any examples the students may have missed. Finally, play the tape once more so the students can hear the examples again in context.

A similar activity can be carried out more formally by adding an extra section to a worksheet (see Figure 31). Students listen again, and against each of their answers (in this case about the life expectancy of human beings) they put the actual words that expressed the speaker's doubt or certainty of the accuracy of the information he was giving — 'probably', 'we can't be a hundred per cent sure' etc.

On the 'Potato Crisps' worksheet (Figure 15) there is a dotted line above each of the boxes that shows a step in the process. When the students have finished listening for information on what happens at each of these stages, they can go back and listen for the time words that introduced each stage — 'next', 'then', 'after that' etc. These can then be written on the dotted line to provide the students with a permanent record of the important language, in addition to the information collected.

By careful use of exercises such as these you may incidentally consolidate or add to the stock of language that the students 'know'. This will mean that in future listening·experiences they can rely a little more on what they 'know' and a little less on strategies for coping with difficulties caused by 'not knowing'. This, in turn, should help them concentrate more on the *message* — the main aim of most real listening.

12 Listening exercises — exercises to help students cope with the sound of English

These exercises are put under two headings:

1 *Indirect practice*   Here you give students practical things to do, but do not give them any explicit teaching about the skills they are supposed to be practising. These exercises do not need any special grounding in phonetics as far as the teacher is concerned.

2 *Practice needing some special training*   Here the students are trained to recognise such things as stressed syllables, to locate nuclear syllables and to pay attention to intonation. These exercises will not suit all students, but those from language backgrounds where intonation and stress are used in very different ways from the way they are used in English (Chinese-speaking students, for example) will almost certainly need the explicit training that these exercises give.

12.1 Indirect practice — pre-listening

1 Written *gap-filling* exercises done on a short section of a text which is about to be heard have been mentioned in Chapter 11, as a way of helping students to sort out problems with

vocabulary in a listening passage. In this case, the deleted words were nouns, verbs, adjectives and adverbs.

Another use of gap-filling is to help students hear the unstressed parts of an utterance more easily, or to help them disentangle words in which there is a lot of elision or assimilation. When you are preparing your lesson, listen to a few sentences of your passage with a tapescript in front of you. Mark on the tapescript all those words which are indistinctly pronounced. Choose from these words some which it would be easy to guess from the context. You can now produce a worksheet with the sentences written on it, but with the indistinct words deleted. Alternatively, you could simply write the gapped sentences on the board before the students hear the tape.

Figure 32 gives an idea of how such sentences might look. Ask the students to suggest what the missing words might be by using the context. You could do this as a class activity or ask students to start off working alone and then to compare their answers with a partner. Grammatical words (prepositions,

Figure 32   Pre-listening gap-filling exercise to sharpen perception of unstressed grammatical words.

You are going to hear these sentences in the listening passage. Before you listen, try to guess what the missing words are. Write them on your worksheet, then compare your answers with your neighbour.

'...................... most alarming thing .... that ....
car just kept on going. There .... nothing ....
could do. I just sat there .... prayed.'

(Note in Teacher's book:
answers: *The, was, the, was I, and* pronounced / ðə /, / wəz /,
/ ðə /, / wəz /, / aɪ /, / m /)

---

articles, pronouns, etc) are much easier to guess than content words, providing you know your grammar! This type of work has the useful spin-off of providing some revision for those whose grammar may be a little shaky, although this is not its main purpose. By doing this guessing work before they hear the passage, students will have certain expectations about what they will hear, and will therefore be much more likely to recognise even very minimally-pronounced words. Of course, you should not give them the right answers before they hear the passage, but leave them to listen for themselves and check their guesses.

2 Asking students to do short *dictations*, taken from *natural* speech can be an excellent way of opening up a discussion about listening problems. I mentioned in Chapter 5.3 the students who thought my heavily-aspirated initial /t/ sound was an /st/. This was revealed through a dictation exercise, and the remedy was direct — to point out that what they had heard was in fact one sort of English /t/, and to demonstrate it several times, using other words they knew (/ 'teɪbɫ / , / 'tuː /, / 'terəbəl / etc). This made these students aware of the problem and put them on the alert for future occurences of this sound.

Another thing that frequently happens in dictations is that students leave out words. These are often the unstressed grammatical words mentioned above — more evidence that they find these difficult to hear.

3 Ask students to *repeat back* to you short snatches of speech as a way of checking what they are hearing. You should ignore the normal detailed inaccuracy of pronunciation of some sounds (/ 'fɪŋkɪŋ / for / 'θɪŋkɪŋ/, for example). Look beyond these for evidence of whole words being lost — 'I want hat, please.' instead of, 'I want a hat, please.' or, 'I like a coke, please.' for, 'I'd like a coke, please.' You will probably find similar mistakes to those made in dictations. Do not use this technique in an inquisitorial way. It is not a sort of test, but one way in which

you might help students to realise and diagnose their listening problems with unstressed words.

12.2 Indirect practice — post-listening

1 Another possible use for *dictation* work is after the students have heard a passage and have understood its content fairly well. Let them work with the tape, either with individual cassette recorders or in a language laboratory, pausing and rewinding as they need. The aim is for them to produce an accurate transcript of a small section of it. (The whole thing is usually too long.) They can check this afterwards against a correct tapescript, and need only refer to the teacher in cases where they do not understand the discrepancies between their version and the 'official' one. This type of work reinforces the ability to expect, and therefore to notice, the small grammatical words, as well as providing useful revision of some of the language items in the passage.

2 *Speaking in unison* with a native speaker is intended to give the learner more empathy with the way in which English is produced, particularly with its rhythm, rather than to improve pronunciation, although this might also happen. The idea of increasing empathy is that it could help to overcome some of the problems mentioned in Chapter 5.3, in which students could not imagine that there was room for so many little syllables squashed between the stressed syllables.

For this exercise, students need individual tape recorders which, ideally, should be fitted with headphones which allow them to listen to their own voices as well as to the tape ('Audio Active' headphones). A language laboratory may also be used. A tape is played, and the learner follows it on a transcript which has been provided. He tries to read aloud in unison with the speaker on the tape. In order to keep up, he will have to try to squash his unstressed syllables in a similar way to the native speaker. Even if he fails he will have had direct experience of the problem and will thus be more aware of the phenomena of connected speech in English. Students who succeed will have gained dividends for their own pronunciation as well as for their listening.

The best sort of tape to use for this is a monologue, one which is read aloud with a fairly regular rhythm. You can give the students extra help by marking in the stressed syllables for them on the tapescript (see Figure 33).

One set of published materials which is very useful for this sort of paced reading is *Stress Time* (Mortimer 1976). This contains simple dialogues and monologues with the stresses marked in. There is even a metronome beating in the background to help the students keep time!

3 Most students are very happy to be able to *follow a tapescript* so that they can simply listen to the tape while following the words on the printed page. This should not be encouraged too much, since they will tend to rely on this help rather than on their ears, but it does have a part to play. What they seem to appreciate is the chance to match up what might seem unfamiliar sounds with the written words, with which they may be quite familiar. Comments such as, 'Can you really pronounce ⎯⎯ like that?' suggest that students do make quite a number of important discoveries for themselves.

Figure 33   Paced reading exercise.

Listen to the speaker on the tape and read aloud with him. The stressed syllables are marked to help you.

'The <u>fact</u> of the <u>matter</u> is he isn't very <u>good</u> at his <u>job.</u> I don't <u>think</u> we can <u>put up</u> with him much <u>longer. Why</u> can't he just <u>go out</u> one <u>day</u> and <u>find</u> something that <u>suits</u> him <u>better</u>?'

12.3 Practice needing some special training

Students can be given a tape and a tapescript and asked to listen and mark in all the stresses. Alternatively, they can be asked to count the unstressed syllables between stresses. This could provide good preparation for a paced reading exercise as described above.

Another, simpler way of working is to ask students to clap or tap out the rhythm of what they hear.

Once students have marked in the stresses on a transcript, they can go back and look for the most prominent or nuclear stresses. This can be useful in cases where you want to point out or discuss the use of contrastive stress, or how given and new information is signalled, as mentioned in Chapter 6.2. If you allow the students to do some of the work themselves, it keeps them more actively involved.

13 Planning listening into your language programme

So far we have looked at listening in isolation. However, it is just as important to plan your course as a whole, term by term, or over the teaching year, as it is to plan individual lessons.

Students need to be able to see some overall direction and purpose in what they are doing, and this involves using all your resource materials, main course book, supplementary materials and your own ideas, in a way that is coherent as well as varied.

13.1 Integrating listening into your main course

Most teachers are working from a main course book, which provides both the syllabus and the backbone of what they do with their classes. How can listening work fit in with this?

Some coursebooks still only provide listening work in the form of dialogues intended as models for speech production. The dangers of relying only on these teaching dialogues to give students listening experience have been pointed out in Chapter 2.1, so these books very definitely need to be supplemented with other listening work. Other courses, such as *Kernel Lessons Plus* (Robert O'Neill, 1973) and *Contemporary English* (Rossner et al, 1979), do contain material specifically designed to improve students' listening skills. In cases like this, you may only have to build in some extensive and out-of-class listening (see Chapter 14) to make sure that your students are given as wide an experience as possible. In either case, the planning problem is how to relate supplementary work to the main course.

Figure 34 sets out a sample plan of how this may be done, using a hypothetical, but fairly typical intermediate textbook as a basis. The notes that follow set out some of the ways in which you can find connections between the main course and other materials.

13.1.1 *Finding links*

Listening work can be linked with your main course in a number of ways:

1 *Through language forms and functions*   You can often find a listening unit which picks up language covered in your main course. *Conversation Pieces* (Mumford, 1983) is an example of listening material whose units have useful structural and functional subheadings, which makes them easy to cross-reference with units in a main course book.

2 *Through subject matter*   You may find listening passages whose subject matter reflects topics covered in your main course. Many published listening materials give topic headings to their units.

3 *Through language skills*   This is a more subtle form of link, but you may, for example, have been doing some work in your main course book on writing summaries from written texts (this is a common form of exam in many school systems). It might be possible to try giving the students a fairly easy listening passage for them to take notes on, and then to see if they were able to produce a summary from these. Interesting discussion of the different problems presented by written and oral texts might follow.

13.1.2 *Finding time*

Many teachers say things like, 'We only have three hours of

English a week. How am I supposed to fit everything in?'

This is a real worry, but it is important to remember that an intensive or an extensive listening experience need not occupy a whole teaching period. Twenty minutes of well-directed intensive listening or five minutes of enjoyable extensive listening, can surely be fitted in from time to time, and will probably do more good than a series of heavy sessions devoted entirely to listening. If you are integrating listening work with your course book, it will also seem less like an interruption and more like a reinforcement of work you are already doing.

You need to strike a balance between too many ties with your main course, which can lead to boredom, and a random choice, which will not give students the sense of direction and purpose they need. Extensive and out-of-class listening can be a very good source of experiences which go beyond the limits of the subject matter highlighted in your course. Unusual and exciting subjects and tasks can be brought in in this part of the course — going to see an English film or play for example, or reading students an exciting adventure story taken from one of the easy levels of a graded readers series.

In order to plan ahead what listening work you can integrate into your course, it helps to start by writing out the important features of each unit of your main course, as shown in Figure 34, under the headings of language, topic and skills. This will help you to spot the potential links between your course book and the listening materials you have under review. Next to each unit's work, and the divisions showing how many lessons you expect to spend on it, you can write in your ideas for extensive and intensive listening work.

Figure 34 is an attempt to reflect a fairly typical situation. A ten-week term, of three lessons per week, is assumed. The average rate of progress is one unit per week. Next to this I have written some suggestions for selections from real published listening materials, with notes on the reasons for my choice. I

Figure 34 Linking listening with a main course book. Plan for a term's teaching of an intermediate level (three lessons a week).

Week	Lesson	Main course units	Intensive listening	Extensive listening
1	1 2 3	**1)** *Describing people* Talking about your family and friends	Nothing in the 1st week. The listening in the course book is good. Concentrate on interesting students in extensive listening.	5-10 minutes, one lesson a week (eg one episode of 'Coke' *Kernel Lessons Intermediate* or sections of graded reader read aloud or on tape)
2	1 2 3	**2)** *Asking for information (1)* Street directions Prepositional phrases	Communication games in pairs (see Rixon, *How to use games in language teaching*) Picture dictations involving prepositional phrases.	
3	1 2 3	**3)** *Understanding instructions* (Reading work on recipes, how to mend a puncture etc)	John Field *Listening Comprehension*, Unit 8. Revises week 1 and gives practice in understanding instructions.	
4	1 2 3	**4)** *Describing places* (including letter-writing about home town)	No intensive listening this week. Written work in course book should be done in class therefore time consuming.	5 minutes in which you tell your students informally about your home town.
5	1 2 3	**5)** *Asking for information (2)* (Times of trains etc.) A short simple unit so there is time for a whole listening lesson.	Use Conversation pieces Susan Mumford, Unit 2 as revision and extension of language in week 1.	

6	1 2 3	6) Invitations	Listening Comprehension – Unit 7 - train times. Extension & revision of language of Unit 5 of main course book. (20 mins)	Extensive listening moved to Wednesday as Friday taken up with jigsaw listening.
7	1 2 3	7) Making arrangements Describing where and when to meet.	Listening Links Unit as a jigsaw activity. This will take a whole lesson. (Friday)	
8	1 2 3	8) Giving reasons/excuses (refer back to jigsaw listening for excuses given for not meeting)	No intensive listening – main course book unit is too long and complicated	Try to bring the language of making arrangements (Unit 7) into the classroom – arranging homework etc.
9	1 2 3	9) Talking about processes How coffee is made & writing exercise	Begin more detailed ear training. Pre-listening gap-filling (see page 107) on 3 minute tape of natural speech. (15 mins)	Tell a short joke (2 mins) in which someone is explaining why he did not do something.
10	1 2 3	10) Guessing & asking for help Difficult reading passage. Students guess what they can and then practise asking the teacher.	Pre-listening gap-filling for prediction of vocabulary items from context (see page 102). This links with the reading passage in the main course unit.	

have also made suggestions for live listening activities which could involve, for example, communication games, or the teacher speaking directly to the class.

Your own plan does not have to be so explicitly expressed, unless you are planning a course with other teachers, in which case they will need to understand the thinking behind your suggestions.

13.2 Integrating listening with other language skills

Listening can play its part in lessons in which a number of other language abilities are being exercised. Three uses of listening in such integrated skills lessons will be looked at:
1 Listening as an input to another activity
2 Listening as a stimulus
3 Jigsaw listening

13.2.1 *Listening as an input*

A listening passage, such as 'Potato Crisps' (Figure 15), can be used as a source of information when you want to give students practice in writing factual accounts. Notes taken from the listening passage can be re-worked into full written form, and you can do useful work on the differences between the spoken and the written form of the same information.

Intensive listening can also supply some of the background information that students need in order to carry out a role-play or a simulation successfully. *Hearsay* (Wellman, 1982) provides materials for listening followed by role-play.

In the popular type of simulation, in which students are asked to discuss possible solutions to some social problem, some of the background can be given through listening. A talk describing the situation could be given live, or students could hear a set of recorded interviews with different people involved in the situation (see Further Reading, ELTI *Simulations*).

13.2.2 *Listening as a stimulus*

Listening is often used to provide *facts* with which students can work, but listening can also provide a *stimulus* — something to react to or against, to set students thinking along particular lines or put them in a particular mood.

If learners are going to discuss or write about a controversial subject, for example, they may find it interesting to start off by hearing some English speakers' views. These can be given as short statements or interviews, recorded by you as suggested in Chapter 3.3. It is best if the views are contrasting, and if they do not present great language difficulties for the students. This allows them to react directly to the message, and to find a speaker with whom they agree or disagree. An example of material that uses interviews on controversial subjects is *Something to Talk About* (Peaty, 1981).

Another way in which listening can be used to evoke a response from students, is when you wish to put them in the right mood or frame of mind to respond to a piece of literature. The use of a song to introduce a literary theme is shown very interestingly in *Between the Lines* (Boardman and McRea, 1984). A Cat Stevens pop song starts off a unit concerning family relations, as seen by writers such as D H Lawrence.

13.2.3 *Jigsaw listening*

This is a specific technique invented by Marion Geddes and Gill Sturtridge (*Listening Links*, 1979).

In this type of work, listening is used as an input to a discussion that revolves around trying to solve a problem or complete a partial story given on tape. The puzzle is set up because none of the students hear the complete information to start with, but have to exchange information with each other to arrive at the full picture.

The procedure is shown in Figure 35. Students start off in three groups. Each group listens to a different tape. Each tape refers to the same situation or story, but gives slightly different information from that on the other tapes — three different eye witnesses' accounts of an accident or a crime, for example. Some information will be common to all tapes, but some may have details not given by others. Some may even contradict information given on other tapes.

Each group listens to its own tape and notes down the relevant information, often helped by a worksheet. Members of each group discuss this information to make sure that everyone has as complete a set of information as possible. Usually they will need to hear the tape several times. This can be done by each group sitting round its own tape recorder or in a language laboratory.

This initial grouping is then split up and students meet each other in new groups as shown in Figure 35. Every new group contains representatives from each of the original groups. Some students find it less nerve-wracking if they can go into the new group with a friend from their original group. This also gets round the problem of classes with awkward numbers of students in them — two students can go into the new group together.

The new groups have to share the different information that they have and try to arrive at the solution, or the most complete version of the story possible. Because gaps and conflicts in information have been built into the materials, the discussion should provide excellent practice of the sort of listening mentioned on page 95, in which the listeners are encouraged to query conflicts and contradictions in what they hear.

At the end of the lesson each group can briefly report back on its conclusions to the rest of the class, so that they can compare versions of the story. Very often, there is a fourth tape, which everyone can hear together. This reveals the end of the story or the answer to the problem, so that everyone goes away satisfied and able to judge for himself how close he and his group came to solving the puzzle.

Figure 35 Organising a Jigsaw listening lesson.

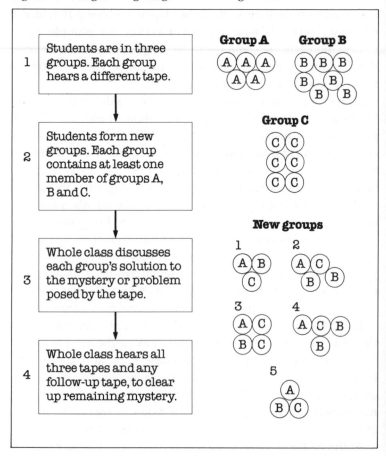

14 Encouraging students to listen by themselves

Ironically, the aim of most good teaching is to help students develop to a point where they are independent of the teacher's help. This is particularly the case with listening. It is one of the main ways in which a learner can 'tune in' by himself to a foreign society when he visits or goes to live in it. It is also the most private and least tangible of the four language skills. You can investigate a learner's writing or speaking difficulties to some extent, and observe how he reads, but what goes on inside each listener's head is more of a mystery. Each learner is on his own in the final analysis, and materials and techniques which can increase his autonomy rather than his loneliness are needed.

14.1 Self-access work

An increasing number of teaching institutions are providing students with more freedom — a choice of materials to work with and space and time to work in, without the direct guidance of the teacher.

The students are given the chance to decide for themselves what will be interesting or useful and to work by themselves. These are both valuable steps towards increased autonomy and away from the traditional dominance of the teacher in the learning process.

Providing self-access facilities requires finance, efficient organisation, and a wealth of materials to choose from. This chapter is therefore mostly directed towards teachers working in institutions where cooperation amongst colleagues is normal and adequate resources are available. The timetable also needs to be planned to allow students time to use the facilities, either within or outside official school hours.

14.1.1 *Advantages of self-access work*

Passages which will interest students, but which are too long to be practical for presentation to the whole class, can be made available — whole talks, radio programmes, etc.

If there is a wide range of subject matter, most students will find something that appeals to them personally. Self-access listening is particularly valuable where students have different backgrounds and specialised interests. This is the case with many *English for Specific Purposes* courses, but more everyday tastes can also be catered for — different hobbies, for example.

If the subjects of the passages are genuinely interesting, the students will be motivated to tackle even something very difficult, because they want to get at the content. A hard-won success is a powerful motivator.

14.1.2 *Equipment and materials*

There are three conditions necessary for a successful self-access listening centre:
1 Abundance of material
2 A good retrieval system
3 Support for students' efforts
   A bank of materials containing only ten or fifteen tapes

presents no real choice. Sooner or later everyone is forced to listen to the same few passages. Real choice cannot start until you reach fifty or so possibilities. This may seem daunting in terms of time and money, but it explains why this chapter is directed towards institutions rather than struggling individual teachers.

Suitable published material can be bought or you could make your own. The expenditure of time and effort should be seen as an investment for the many years of use a successful listening library will give.

Once about fifty tapes have been collected and processed (see Figure 36) the library can start to be used while other tapes are added more gradually.

Figure 36   Catalogue entry.

Title of tape Synthetic Protein

Code number of tape Biol no 45

Topic The production of synthetic proteins from beans.
How they can be made suitable for people to eat.

Setting/type of talk Taped during a real seminar in Belfast.
The main speaker, Dr Brown, is interrupted from time by requests for clarification by students. Most of what Dr Brown says is about **Processes of Manufacture**.

Characteristics of speaker Dr Brown is speaking without notes and there are many hesitations, repetitions and places where he changes his mind about what to say.

Length of tape 6½ minutes.

Accompanying materials 1. transcript 2. diagram showing main outline of the talk, to be used for guided note taking 3. glossary of technical terms used by Dr Brown.

The retrieval system involves both the way the tapes are stored and the way they are catalogued. It is useless to present students with hundreds of tapes without giving them any idea of what they contain or where they can be found. Each tape should have its own section in the catalogue which gives the information shown in Figure 36. Each tape needs a code number which indicates where it is stored. This should be repeated in the catalogue and on any support materials that go with it.

If your collection of tapes can be divided naturally into different topics, you could prefix the number with the topic name or, more briefly, a letter showing to which group the tape belongs — G for Geology, A for Architecture. Colour coding — blue labels for medical topics, red for humour — could also be used.

Your catalogue should have a plan of the storage system attached to it, to show where each tape and its accompanying materials can be found (see Figure 37). A loose-leaf file is an ideal container for the catalogue sheets, since alterations and additions can easily be made. You should put a contents list at the front of the file, listing all the categories of tape. This makes it easy for students to find the topics they are interested in. An efficient catalogue enables students to find what they want without having to ask the teacher for too much help, and if the storage area is well planned and the labels clear, the students can be trusted (or trained!) to put materials back in the right place after use. This will save you a lot of 'housekeeping' work.

Classroom listening activities tend to be directed by the teacher. Even when students listen privately for part of the time, this is only because the teacher has planned it that way. In self-access listening the teacher uses no such control, but he does still have a responsibility to help students to find ways of working that suit them.

Written materials which accompany the tape can suggest a number of different activities which students can choose from. They can also remind them to use techniques learned in class —

Figure 37 Storage layout for tapes and accompanying materials.

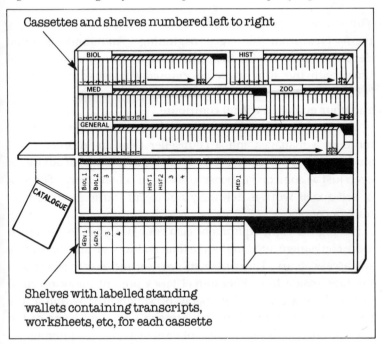

Cassettes and shelves numbered left to right

BIOL | HIST | MED | ZOO | GENERAL

BIOL 1 | BIOL 2 | 3 | HIST 1 | HIST 2 | 3 | 4 | MED 1

GEN 1 | GEN 2 | 3 | 4

CATALOGUE

Shelves with labelled standing
wallets containing transcripts,
worksheets, etc, for each cassette

using the pause and rewind buttons, for example — to make
things easier for themselves.

Worksheets can also help the students understand the tapes
more easily. Diagrams such as that in Figure 38 set out the outline
of what they are going to hear. They know how many sections
there will be and what the main points will be.

Transcripts should be provided for each tape in the collection.
Many students will at first want only to sit and listen and read
along. As I have suggested in Chapter 12.2, this seems a rather
unenterprising activity but does have its own value, although it
would be good if students could be persuaded to try some
different activities as well.

14.2 Autonomy for the students

You cannot expect all students to be able to work well by themselves from the very beginning. Autonomy is often developed from having the right amount of support at the right time, with the support being gradually lessened as students become more confident. A good catalogue, usable worksheets and your guidance will all contribute.

The teacher's role changes in self-access work. He becomes more of a manager and a counsellor than an informant. All students need the teacher to be available as a source of advice, or even just as someone to boast to about an achievement. The idea of self-access work is definitely not to cut learners off from all human contact.

Having the right equipment also counts. Cassettes are much more convenient and tangle-free than reel-to-reel tape for use in a self-access library. The containers are neat and easy to label (label the tape inside too). Reel-to-reel tapes present many practical problems, but they will probably be superseded within a few years anyway. Figure b in the Appendix sets out some of the advantages and disadvantages of various types of equipment.

Make sure that when a listening task involves searching for pieces of information, there is an answer sheet that the student can find easily for himself. Another loose-leaf binder, with all the answer keys in it, can be kept next to the main catalogue. Students will then need to consult the teacher only in cases where they do not understand why a certain answer is wrong or right, and will be independent as far as checking routine answers is concerned.

Figure 38 illustrates the type of instruction sheet and range of tasks that has been found useful with adult students. For younger students, you can make tasks requiring less time and concentrated effort.

Even if the facilities you have in your school do not permit you to set up a complete self-access listening library, you could still get together a collection of tapes which could be kept in a cupboard. If you have no individual cassette recorders and no language laboratory in your school, you could set up a lending system, so that students could sign for a tape and take it home to listen to.

Figure 38   Accompanying materials for 'Synthetic Protein'.

Main outline of talk:

Use this diagram to help you to find your way through the tape.

1 Dr Brown explains how protein   Your notes
   is made from beans.
   (*Student interrupts*)

   ↓

2 Dr Brown talks about bean
   protein as food substitute.
   (*Student interrupts*)

   ↓

2 Dr Brown talks about its use
   in school dinners.
   (*Student makes a joke*)

Suggested activities:

Without using the tapescript

1 Write down the names of the two types of bean protein
   mentioned by Dr Brown.
2 Draw a diagram to represent the process of making bean
   protein described by Dr Brown.

Following the tapescript

3 Check your answers to questions 1 and 2.
4 Listen once more, following on the tapescript.

14.3 Listening outside the school

Most educational systems teach foreign languages with the hope that learners will be able to use them in real life at some point. Not everyone will have the chance to go abroad, or even to use the language often within his own country, but opportunities do exist to listen to English in a pleasurable or useful way.

Pop music and English language films are obvious links with the English speaking world. English radio broadcasts can be picked up in most parts of the world, and embassies and cultural centres often provide the chance to get in touch with other English users.

For teachers working with students within the United Kingdom, the opportunities to use English outside school are huge, but those working abroad need not despair either. There are two ways in which you can encourage students to listen outside the school. The first is to get students to *exercise* their listening outside school and the second is about finding opportunities for listening for *pleasure*. The hope is that useful enjoyable exercise may lead to spontaneous listening for pure pleasure.

14.3.1 *Listening assignments outside the school*

Self-access listening has been discussed as a stepping stone between listening guided by the teacher and greater independence. Students who have met certain types of listening experiences in the listening library may feel prepared to try them in their own time. Radio programmes are an obvious example. Although it is not practical to expect a whole class to be able to listen to a particular BBC World Service programme, it is worthwhile referring occasionally to items you may have heard and encouraging students to use the radio to give them listening practice (see Tomalin 1986).

Opportunities for work involving live listening vary from place to place. Obviously learners on a course in the United Kingdom can more easily be asked to prepare a questionnaire to use with native speaker 'victims' than can students in Poland or Thailand. However, individual teachers use their ingenuity (and their contacts) in a surprising number of ways. I recently heard an Italian teacher of English explain how she had obtained the permission of different embassies in Rome for her students to visit them, armed with questionnaires about how their staff had settled down in Italy. Not all of these embassies belonged to English-speaking countries, but English served as a lingua franca between students and interviewees. In China, I remember being interviewed in my hotel garden by some very charming university students who had been given the project of finding a tourist and asking about his or her impressions of the town.

In the United Kingdom, I have given students simple projects such as ringing up the various recorded telephone services, like the weather, the traffic reports or even the recipe of the day. It is more demanding to ask them to ring the live information services, such as directory enquiries or train timetable information, to find out specific things. It should be stressed that this should only be done when someone actually needs some information of the kind, or you may find your school receiving indignant letters from British Telecom!

14.3.2 Listening for pleasure outside the school

Again opportunities for making contact with the language outside the school will vary, as will the amount of enthusiasm shown by students about non-obligatory, 'extra-mural' listening. Students have a perfect right not to be keen, but you should be equipped with good information on what is available should they relent! You need to do some research into:

1 what English language broadcasting stations can be received.
2 what English language film showings are available.
3 what social or cultural clubs are open to students of English language.
4 where records and cassettes can be bought or borrowed.

Your local British Embassy information office, consulate or British Council office should be able to help. Most British Council libraries have a recorded sound section from which tapes and records of plays, poetry, songs and recordings of popular radio programmes can be borrowed. The BBC publication 'London Calling' can also be obtained from British Council offices and consulates. This contains details of all the BBC World Service broadcasts and their radio frequencies for each country.

If you prepare a short handout on all the possibilities, no one who wishes to extend his listening experience into his private life need miss an opportunity.

This has been the aim of this book, to describe activities that start within the school or the class, but which will lead the learner nearer and nearer the stage at which he becomes no longer a struggling learner but simply a *listener*.

Appendix

Figure a Recording your own materials.

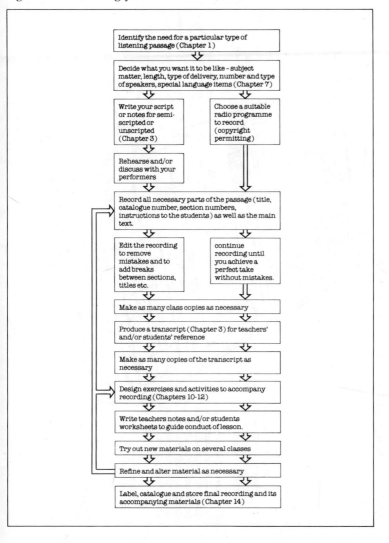

Figure b Ideal playback machine for teachers' use.

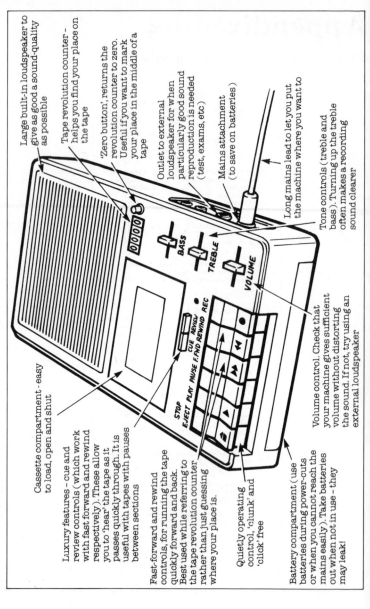

Cassette compartment - easy to load, open and shut

Large built-in loudspeaker to give as good a sound-quality as possible

Tape revolution counter - helps you find your place on the tape

'Zero button'; returns the revolution counter to zero. Useful if you want to mark your place in the middle of a tape

Outlet to external loudspeaker for when particularly good sound reproduction is needed (test, exams, etc)

Mains attachment (to save on batteries)

Long mains lead to let you put the machine where you want to

Tone controls (treble and bass). Turning up the treble often makes a recording sound clearer

Luxury features - cue and review controls (which work with fast forward and rewind respectively). These allow you to 'hear' the tape as it passes quickly through. It is useful with tapes with pauses between sections

Fast-forward and rewind controls, for running the tape quickly forward and back. Best used while referring to the tape revolution counter rather than just guessing where your place is.

Quietly operating control, 'chunk' and 'click' free

Battery compartment (use batteries during power-cuts or when you cannot reach the mains easily). Take batteries out when not in use - they may leak!

Volume control. Check that your machine gives sufficient volume without distorting the sound. If not, try using an external loudspeaker

Further reading

The British Council (1978) *ELT Documents Special—The Teaching of Listening Comprehension* Pergamon, Oxford

Brown, G (1977) *Listening to Spoken English* Longman, London

Brown, G and Yule, G (1983) *Teaching the Spoken Language* Cambridge University Press, Cambridge

Clark, H H and Clark, E V (¹977) *Psychology and Language: Introduction to Psycholinguistics* Harcourt Brace Jovanovich, New York

Coulthard, M; Brazil, D and Johns, C (1980) *Discourse Intonation and Language Teaching* Longman, London

McDonough, S (1981) *Psychology in Foreign Language Teaching* Allan & Unwin, London

Munby, J (1978) *Communicative Syllabus Design* Cambridge University Press, Cambridge

Rixon, S (1981) *How to use games in language teaching* Macmillan, Basingstoke

Roach, P (1983) *English phonetics and phonology; a practical course* Cambridge University Press, Cambridge

Tench, P (1981) *Pronunciation skills* Macmillan, Basingstoke

Tomalin, B (1986) *Video, TV and radio in the English class* Macmillan, Basingstoke

Trudgill, P and Hughes, A (1979) *English Accents and Dialects* Edward Arnold, London

Williams, E (1984) *Reading in the language classroom* Macmillan, Basingstoke

Coursebooks

Blundell, L and Stokes, J (1981) *Task Listening* Cambridge University Press, Cambridge

Boardman, R and McRae, J (1984) *Between the Lines* Cambridge University Press, Cambridge

Field, J (1983) *Listening Comprehension* Macmillan, London

Geddes, M and Sturtridge, G (1979) *Listening Links* Heinemann, London

Mumford, S (1983) *Conversation Pieces* Pergamon, Oxford

O'Neill, R (1973) *Kernel Lessons Plus* Longman, London

O'Neill, R; Kingsbury, R and Yeadon, T (1971) *Kernel Lessons Intermediate* Longman, London

Peaty, D (1981) *Something to Talk About* Nelson, Walton-on-Thames

Rossner et al (1979) *Contemporary English* Macmillan, London

Wellman, G (1982) *Hearsay* Nelson, Walton-on-Thames

Index

List of phonetic symbols

Consonants		Vowels	
p	pad	iː	see
b	big	ɪ	it
t	too	e	get
d	dog	æ	cat
k	keep	ɑː	father
g	go	ɒ	hot
tʃ	chin	ɔː	saw
dʒ	jam	ʊ	put
f	fish	uː	too
v	vase	ʌ	up
θ	thin	ɜː	bird
ð	then	ə	driver, China
s	sit	eɪ	day
z	zero	əʊ	go
ʃ	ship	aɪ	fly
ʒ	measure	aʊ	how
h	hot	ɔɪ	boy
m	man	ɪə	here
n	no	eə	there
ŋ	long	ʊə	poor
l	leg		
ɫ	table	ʔ	glottal stop
r	red		
j	yes		
w	win		